**WHAT THE CRITICS SAY:**

*A very worthwhile addition to any travel library.* —WCBS Newsradio

*Armed with these guides, you may never again stay in a conventional hotel.*
—Travelore Report

*Easily carried ... neatly organized ... wonderful. A helpful addition to my travel library. The authors wax as enthusiastically as I do about the almost too-quaint-to-believe Country Inns.* —San Francisco Chronicle

*One can only welcome such guide books and wish them long, happy, and healthy lives in print.* —Wichita Kansas Eagle

*This series of pocket-sized paperbacks will guide travelers to hundreds of little known and out of the way inns, lodges, and historic hotels.... a thorough menu.*
—(House Beautiful's) Colonial Homes

*Charming, extremely informative, clear and easy to read; excellent travelling companions.* —Books-Across-The-Sea *(The English Speaking Union)*

*... a fine selection of inviting places to stay... provide excellent guidance....*
—Blair & Ketchum's Country Journal

*Obviously designed for our kind of travel.... [the authors] have our kind of taste.*
—Daily Oklahoman

*The first guidebook was so successful that they have now taken on the whole nation.... Inns are chosen for charm, architectural style, location, furnishings and history.* —Portland Oregonian

*Many quaint and comfy country inns throughout the United States... The authors have a grasp of history and legend.* —Dallas (Tx.) News

*Very fine travel guides.* —Santa Ana (Calif.) Register

*A wonderful source for planning trips.* —Northampton (Mass.) Gazette

*... pocketsize books full of facts.... attractively made and illustrated.*
—New York Times Book Review

*Hundreds of lovely country inns reflecting the charm and hospitality of various areas throughout the U.S.* —Youngstown (Ohio) Vindicator

*Some genius must have measured the average American dashboard, because the Compleat Traveler's Companions fit right between the tissues and bananas on our last trip.... These are good-looking books with good-looking photographs.... very useful.*

—East Hampton (N.Y.) Star

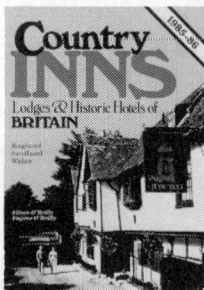

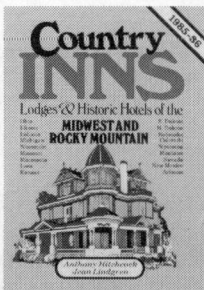

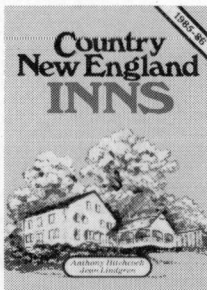

# California, Oregon, & Washington

## COUNTRY INNS
### Lodges & Historic Hotels

BURT FRANKLIN & COMPANY

Published by
BURT FRANKLIN & COMPANY
P.O. Box 856
New York, New York 10014, U.S.A.

**TWELFTH EDITION**

*Library of Congress Cataloging in Publication Data*

Country inns, lodges, and historic hotels
of California & the West

(The Compleat traveler's companion)
Includes index.
1. Hotels, taverns, etc. — California — Directories.
2. Hotels, taverns, etc. — West (U.S.) — Directories.
II. Title.III.
Series.
TX907.H537    1990    647'.947901
ISBN 0-89102-427-1 (pbk.)

Cover illustration courtesy of
The Gosby House Inn
Pacific Grove, California

Manufactured in the United States of America

1 3 4 2

# Contents

# Introduction

In this new edition, we have quoted the most recent room rates in a combined rate chart and index at the end of the book. Readers should note that the listed rates are *subject to change*. While the quoted rates are for double occupancy in most cases, single travelers as well as larger groups should inquire about special rates. We list daily room rates as based on the American Plan (AP, all three meals included), Modified American Plan (MAP, breakfast and dinner included), Bed and Breakfast (BB, either full or Continental breakfast included), or European Plan (EP, no meals). In many cases a tax and a service charge will be added. Be sure to ask. Children and pets present special problems for many inns. If either is *not* welcome at an inn it is noted in the description. These regulations also often change, and it is imperative that families traveling with either inquire in advance. Though many inns state they are open all year, we find that many close during slow periods. Call first to confirm your room reservations.

The inns described in this book were chosen for their inherent charm, based partially on their architectural style, location, furnishings, and history. We have made every effort to provide information as carefully and accurately as possible, but we remind readers that all listed rates and schedules are subject to change. Further, we have neither solicited nor accepted any fees or gratuities for being included in this book or any of the other books in this series. We have tried to be responsive to reader suggestions arising out of earlier editions of this book. Should readers wish to offer suggestions for future editions, we welcome their correspondence.

# California

## GARRATT MANSION

900 Union Street, Alameda, CA 94501. 415-521-4779. *Innkeepers:* Betty and Royce Gladden. Open all year.

Alameda is a small island just ten miles from San Francisco and Berkeley, a place where guests can bicycle easily from one end to the other or take evening walks along the beaches. Innkeeper Betty Gladden grew up in the Bay area, has spent twenty years on the island, and is an expert on its people and its offerings.

Garratt Mansion is an 1893 Victorian manor house that displays quality workmanship in its extensive carved woods, panelling, polished open beams of redwood and oak, and leaded-glass windows decorated with prisms and stained glass. The second floor houses a guest living room and a sitting room on the balcony. The four guest rooms on the third floor have sweeping views. Fresh flowers abound inside and out. Hand-embroidered pillow cases are ironed, and sheets are line-dried. The weather determines the afternoon beverages and snacks — cool days bring hot chocolate and cookies by the fireside, while hot afternoons offer iced tea or lemonade served with mint.

*Accommodations:* 6 rooms, 3 with private bath. *Pets and smoking:* Not permitted. *Driving Instructions:* Ask for instructions when making reservations.

CALIFORNIA

SCALE OF MILES

0  10  20  30  50        75

ONE INCH EQUALS APPROXIMATELY 45 MILES

NEVADA

CASCADE RANGE

SHASTA NAT'L REC AREA

LASSEN VOLCANIC NAT'L PK

Requa

Eureka
Ferndale

Garberville

Westport
Fort Bragg
Mendocino
Little River
Elk
Boonville
Gualala

Sea Ranch
Cloverdale
Geyserville
Jenner
Guerneville
Pt. Reyes
Olema
Sausalito
Half Moon

COAST RANGE

French Gulch

Sacramento River

Chico

Wilbur Springs

Healdsburg
Calistoga
Saint Helena
Yountville
Santa Rosa
Sonoma
Napa
Benicia
Pt. Richmond
Berkeley
San Fra
Santa Clara

Quincy
Clio
Downieville

Nevada City
Grass Valley
Auburn

Sacramento

Fairfield

Olympic Valley
Truckee
Tahoe City

Georgetown
Coloma
Placerville

Volcano
Amador City
Sutter Creek
Ione
Jackson
San Andreas
Murphys
Columbia
Jamestown
Groveland
Sonora

Tuolumne

YOSEMITE NAT'L PK

SIERR

Yosemite

Laytonville

Sebastopol

COAST RANGE

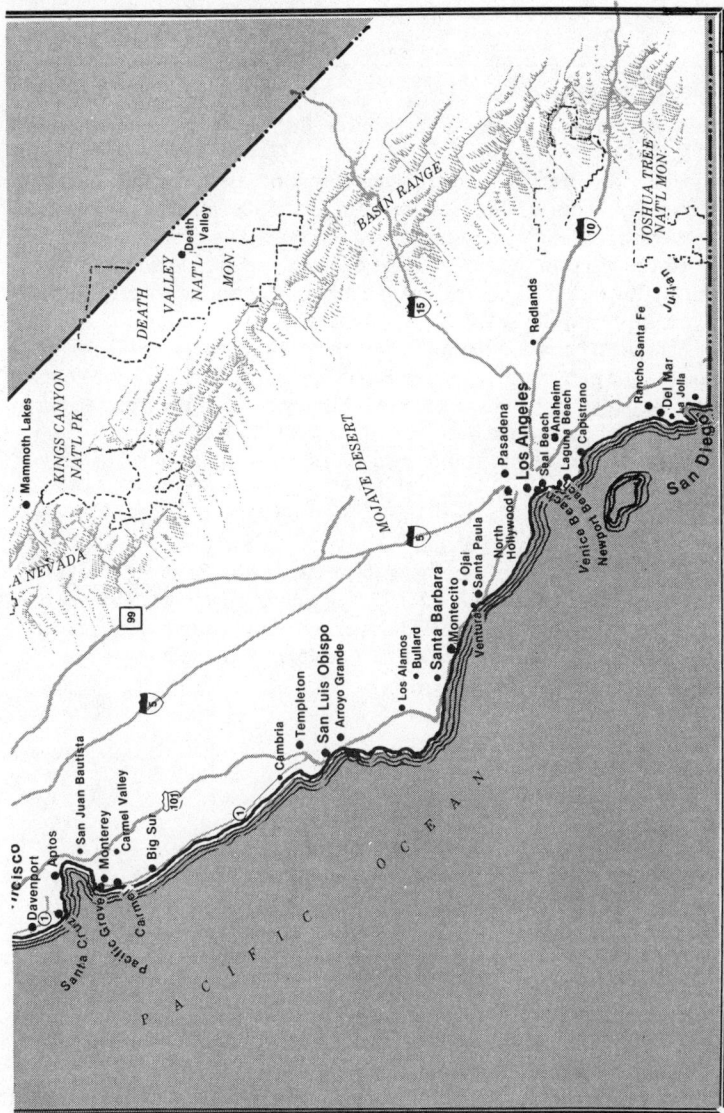

BASIN RANGE

DEATH VALLEY NATL MON.

Death Valley

JOSHUA TREE NATL MON.

10

15

Julian

Redlands

Rancho Santa Fe

Del Mar

La Jolla

San Diego

Mammoth Lakes

KINGS CANYON NATL PK

A NEVADA

MOJAVE DESERT

Pasadena

Los Angeles

Seal Beach

Anaheim

Laguna Beach

Capistrano

99

North Hollywood

Venice Beach

Long Beach

Newport

Ojai

Santa Paula

Ventura

Montecito

Santa Barbara

Los Alamos

Bullard

5

San Luis Obispo

Arroyo Grande

Templeton

Cambria

101

San Juan Bautista

Monterey

Carmel Valley

Big Sur

1

Carmel

cisco

Davenport

Aptos

Santa Cruz

Pacific Grove

PACIFIC OCEAN

## FENSALDEN

33810 Navarro Ridge Road, Albion, California. Mailing address: P.O. Box 99, Albion, CA 95410. 707-937-4042. *Innkeepers:* Fran and Scott Brazil. Open all year; closed occasionally mid-week.

A group of historic buildings, including an 1860s stagecoach stop and a tavern of similar age, were joined to create Fensalden, a peaceful north-coast inn on nearly 20 acres of headland meadows that sweep almost down to the Pacific Ocean. The name Fensalden means "home of the mist and the sea."

Fensalden has a country look, with many antiques and old-fashioned clocks. The parlor and tavern room offer magnificent views, as do the west-facing guest rooms in the main building and in the water tower. Some guest rooms have fireplaces. The Water Tower suite has a kitchenette and a sleeping loft. The east-facing guest rooms have their own balconies and porches. A wood-burning stove and a grand piano await guests in the tavern, where the innkeepers serve breakfast and wine and hors d'oeurves in the evening.

*Accommodations:* 8 rooms with private bath. *Pets and smoking:* Not permitted. *Children:* Under 12 by prior arrangement. *Driving instructions:* One mile south of Albion, on Route 1, turn east on Navarro Ridge road. The inn is the first building on the left.

## MINE HOUSE INN

14125 Route 49, Amador City, California. Mailing address: P.O.
Box 245, Amador City, CA 95601. 209-267-5900. *Innkeepers:* Peter
and Ann Marie Daubenspeck. Open all year.

In the heart of the Mother Lode, Amador City saw the discovery of
gold in its streams in 1849, although the real bonanza — the discovery
of gold-encrusted quartz — came the next year. The Keystone Consoli-
dated Mining Company, originating from this discovery, became one
of the largest gold-quartz claims in the state. When it finally closed,
about $23,500,000-worth had been taken from the mine. About twenty-
five years ago, Peter Daubenspeck discovered the old mining-company
office and began the painstaking conversion of the early building into
an inn.

Guests stay in rooms named for their function in Gold Rush days.
All are furnished with Victorian antiques obtained with 100 miles of
Amador City. The Mill Grinding Room's ceiling still bears supports
for the shafting that drove the machinery used to pulverize sample ore
before assaying. In the Retort Room, gold was smelted into bullion
and carried by dumb-waiter to the vault; today, this is a sitting room
and gallery. Two rooms have balconies overlooking the town and the
old mine frame.

Guests are treated to sweet rolls, coffee, tea, hot chocolate, and
orange juice in their rooms at the start of each morning. No other meals
are served, but guests are directed to local restaurants. A swimming
pool is available for guests' use.

*Accommodations:* 8 rooms with private bath. *Pets:* Not permitted.
*Driving Instructions:* The inn is on Route 49 at the south edge of town.

## Anaheim, California

### ANAHEIM COUNTRY INN

856 South Walnut, Anaheim, CA 92802. 714-778-0150. *Innkeepers:* Lois Ramont and Marilyn Watson. Open all year.

This sturdy house was built in 1910 for John Cook, who became Anaheim's mayor four years later. The mayor loved roses, and here today are a rose garden, an herb garden, and an old-fashioned fern garden surrounded by lawn and avocado trees. Lois and Marilyn have transformed the house into a bed-and-breakfast inn with country Victorian antiques and near antiques of the 1930s and 1940s, striped and flowered wallpapers, Oriental rugs, and lace curtains at big sunny windows. Many rooms have leaded beveled-glass windows that create tiny rainbows when they catch the sun just right. A full breakfast is served in the dining room, and in early evening the innkeepers offer light snacks in the parlor. Paddle fans, old-fashioned print wallpapers, and brass student lamps add homey touches to the upstairs guest rooms. The inn is in a quiet residential area near Disneyland and Knott's Berry Farm, and the Fun Bus stop is just three blocks away.

*Accommodations:* 8 rooms, 4 with private bath. *Pets and smoking:* Not permitted. *Children:* Under 13 not permitted. *Driving Instructions:* Call for detailed instructions.

## COOPER HOUSE BED & BREAKFAST INN

1184 Church Street, Angels Camp, California. Mailing address: P.O. Box 1388, Angels Camp, CA 95222. 209-736-2145. *Innkeepers:* Chris Sears. Open all year.

Angels Camp is in the heart of California's Gold Rush country, close to Big Trees State Park, which has numerous hiking trails amid giant sequoias. One illustrious guest, Mark Twain, wrote "The Jumping Frog of Calaveras County" while in residence here.

Cooper House, a California–Craftsman-style bungalow built in 1911, has furnishings and decor that encompass the years from the early 1900s to the 1940s. Many once belonged to an early Calaveras County family, the Stevenots. The center of activity is the living room, with its unusual greenstone fireplace. Two suites have sitting rooms, one with a garden view and one with its own deck. A full breakfast is served in the dining area, and afternoon refreshments are served on the back patio. A path leads through the garden to a gazebo.

*Accommodations:* 3 rooms with private bath. *Pets and smoking:* Not permitted. *Driving Instructions:* From Route 49 (Main Street) in Angels Camp, turn onto Raspberry Lane. Go 1 block and make a hard left onto Church Street. The inn is the only house on the block.

## THE APPLE LANE INN

6265 Soquel Drive, Aptos, CA 95003. 408-475-6868. *Innkeeper:* Ann Farley. Open all year.

The Apple Lane Inn began as an apple farm in 1876. Today the Victorian farmhouse still stands on three secluded acres of orchards and fields between Aptos and Soquel on the coast of central California with easy reach of the beaches of Monterey Bay and redwood parks.

The wine cellar was turned into a pub where guests can play darts or games or watch T.V. A parlor upstairs is furnished with Victorian pieces and features a player piano and a working fireplace. Outside the house is a patio and grape arbor surrounded by hydrangeas and begonias. The guest rooms have rustic antiques, dhurrie rugs, and stenciled designs on their walls and floors, and home-made quilted pillows on the beds. Sinks have been set into antique commodes in each room. One bathroom has a skylight over a bathtub big enough for two. A full breakfast, including home-baked apple pastries, is served in the parlor. Restaurants are nearby.

*Accommodations:* 5 rooms, 3 with private bath. *Pets:* Not permitted. *Smoking:* Restricted. *Children:* Not permitted. *Driving Instructions:* The inn is south of San Jose, halfway between Soquel and Aptos on Soquel Drive.

## MANGELS HOUSE

570 Aptos Creek Road, Aptos, California. Mailing address: P.O. Box 302, Aptos, CA 95001. 408-688-7982. *Innkeeper:* Jacqueline Fisher. Open all year except December 24 through 26.

Mangels House is a Southern-style mansion built in the 1800s as the seaside home of Claus Mangels, who, with his brother-in-law, Claus Spreckels, founded the sugar-beet industry in California. Mangels House is on four acres of gardens and lawns at the edge of the 10,000-acre Nisene Marks Forest, a redwood preserve with miles of hiking and jogging trails.

The Mangels kept the estate in the family until it was sold to the Fishers in 1979. Today, it is furnished with a variety of antiques. In the evenings, guests gather for aperatifs in the sitting room, which has a rough marble fireplace flanked by overstuffed couches. At one end is a concert grand piano and, at the other, a library and a gaming table. A full breakfast is served in the dining room. The inn has wraparound verandas with swings; the beach is less than a mile away.

*Accommodations:* 5 rooms, 3 with private bath. *Pets and smoking:* Restricted. *Children:* Under 12 not permitted. *Driving Instructions:* From Santa Cruz take Route 1 to the Aptos–Seacliff Beach exit. Go back over the freeway and turn right at the traffic light onto Soquel Drive, 1/3 mile under railway bridge. Turn left on Aptos Creek Road. The inn is 1/2 mile on the right.

*Auburn, California*

## POWER'S MANSION INN

164 Cleveland Avenue, Auburn, CA 95603. 916-885-1166. *Innkeeper:* Judith and Rene Vincent. Open all year.

Auburn, an historic gold-mining town, is the gateway to the majestic Sierra Mountains. The town had been known as "Dry Diggins" in the days of the Gold Rush. Michael Power, caught up in the gold fever, journeyed here in 1854 and made a fortune in the rich Hidden Treasure Mine.

The Power's Mansion is now restored and furnished with four-poster and brass beds, hand-screened Victorian wallpapers, imported fabrics, and American, French, and English antiques. The sitting room has an antique pump organ still in working condition. There are many fireplaces, two in guest suites. A stone terrace, shaded by an old oak, is a favorite spot for breakfast. Terry cloth robes and special soaps are provided for guests. Tea and wine are served in the late afternoon.

*Accommodations:* 13 rooms with private bath. *Pets:* Not permitted. *Driving Instructions:* Take I-80 to the Elm Street exit. Proceed left to High Street and turn right, then left onto Cleveland Street. The driveway to the inn is first on the left.

## UNION HOTEL

401 First Street, Benicia, CA 94510. 707-746-0100. *Innkeeper:* Stephen Lipworth. Open all year.

The Union Hotel, built in 1882, was a twenty-room bordello until the 1950s. A major renovation was completed in 1981, when this sturdy four-square building reopened with a dozen antique-filled guest rooms and a French restaurant that has received national recognition. The superb stained glass in the bar is the work of two area artists, Doug Asheraft and Max Pachner.

Each guest room is distinctly decorated. The Ritz, for example, has Louis XVI furniture including two armoires. Greak Oak is a testimony to the Eastlake period, while Four Poster includes a four-poster bed topped with a lacy, diamond-patterned canopy. Regardless of mood, rooms have queen- or king-size beds, individual room-temperature controls, private baths with Jacuzzi bathtubs, and television, and many have views of the bay.

*Accommodations:* 12 rooms with private bath. *Pets:* Not permitted. *Driving Instructions:* Benicia is on I-780, off I-80 or I-680. Take the Second Street exit, turn left to the first light. Turn right on Military Street and go to First, then left for eight blocks.

*Berkeley, California*

## GRAMMA'S BED AND BREAKFAST INN

2740 Telegraph Avenue, Berkeley, CA 94705. 415-549-2145. *Inn-keeper:* C. L. Runyon. Open all year.

If Gramma's name conjures up images of plump, white-haired ladies in faded washdresses and serviceable aprons, think again. How about a Gramma (more likely called *Grandmère*) ensconced in a turn-of-the-century half-timbered Tudor mansion surrounded by a friendly staff. Imagine rooms with Victorian antiques, Oriental rugs, polished inlaid-oak floors, and leaded-glass windows. This is the Gramma of Berkeley's first bed-and-breakfast inn, located just a few blocks from the university. In all fairness, it must be said that there are always homemade cookies in the cookie jar and a glass of cold milk to accompany them, in true "Gramma" fashion.

Guest rooms are in the main house, in the cottage beyond the English country garden, or in the Jewel Fay House next door. Some have French doors opening onto private decks with garden views; ten have working fireplaces. Hand-made quilts are on brass or heavy antique-walnut bedsteads. There are French armoires and, in some rooms, window seats cushioned in a small floral print matching the wallpaper.

Breakfast, served in breakfast nooks, includes omelets, muffins, assorted pastries, croissants, and homemade preserves, along with fresh fruits and cereals. On Sundays there is a champagne brunch. Two sitting areas downstairs in the main house display splendid plasterwork with ornate ceiling moldings and have Italian hand-painted fireplace tiles. In summer, the garden is a popular spot for outdoor weddings.

*Accommodations:* 30 rooms, 28 with private bath. *Pets and smoking:* Restricted. *Driving Instructions:* Take the Ashby Avenue turnoff to Telegraph. Turn left and go three blocks.

# Big Sur, California

Big Sur is one of the most spectacular parts of the coast between San Francisco and Los Angeles. A trip via Highway 1 through the coastal wilderness will never be forgotten. Travelers are urged to fill their gas tanks before setting out; there are relatively few places to get auto service along this route. Big Sur, which remains largely a protected and undeveloped region, enjoyed some fame in the 1940s and 1950s as the site of an enclave of writers and artists, many of whom had followed the lead of Henry Miller after he moved there as World War II was drawing to a close. *Pfeiffer Big Sur State Park* offers programs that provide an introduction to the redwood and chaparral ecology of the area.

## VENTANA INN

Highway 1, Big Sur, CA 93920. 408-667-2331 or 408-624-4812; toll-free from California only, 1-800-628-6500. *Innkeeper:* Robert E. Bussinger. Open all year.

The Ventana Inn is a strikingly modern (1975) complex that is set in a meadow permanently kept in pasture, 1,200 feet above sea level, amid the spectacular beauty of Big Sur. The buildings comprise an inn, a restaurant, and a country store. Their builders made full use of the warm, clean lines of exposed natural cedar. Within the guest rooms, wooden walls provide the backdrop for king- or queen-size beds with hand-painted, carved arched headboards and handmade Nova Scotian quilts. Many of the rooms have a fireplace, as well as a private dining alcove and wet bar, and there are a few townhouse suites with separate bedrooms, some with private hot tubs. Guests enjoy saunas, Japanese therapeutic hot baths, and two 75-foot heated swimming pools. A Continental breakfast is served in the lobby or on a tray delivered to their rooms, and an elaborate complimentary wine and cheese buffet is set out in the afternoons.

The Ventana's restaurant is a short walk or drive away, at the summit of a low ridge. There, overlooking the sea and surrounded by mountains, diners gather for brunch, lunch, dinner, or supper. The mood is enhanced by the soft classical music played throughout the meals.

A bonus for visitors to the Ventana Inn is its store. Here carefully selected gifts are available. There are a number of kitchen tools, including chef's knives, as well as Pendleton shirts and blankets, imported

buttons, shaving brushes, baskets, and Big Sur honey.

*Accommodations:* 60 rooms with private bath. *Pets:* Not permitted. *Children:* Not encouraged. *Driving Instructions:* The inn is off Highway 1, in Big Sur, 28 miles south of Carmel.

### Boonville, California

## TOLL HOUSE INN

15301 Highway 253, Boonville, California. Mailing address: P.O.
Box 268, Boonville, CA 95415. 707-895-3630. *Innkeeper:* Barbara
McGuinness. Open all year.

The first guests to stay at the Toll House Inn arrived by stagecoach
in 1912. Today, this inland Mendocino County sheep-country inn, surrounded by acres of verdant forests and gentle sloping hills, which many
visitors find reminiscent of Scotland or Wales, continues to welcome
overnight visitors.

The solarium provides an informal dining area and houses the inn's
television set and videotape collection. A more formal dining room
is the scene of specially arranged gourmet dinners with seasonal local
ingredients.

Guests are welcome to gather in the kitchen, where a Franklin stove
keeps away the chill during the winter months. There is a downstairs
guest suite reminiscent of a library that has its own wood-burning fireplace. Upstairs, the Master suite has a tiled fireplace. All rooms are
decorated with carefully chosen colors and fabrics. There is a secluded
hot tub in the garden. Guests may hike, ride, hunt or fish on the adjacent ranch.

*Accommodations:* 5 rooms, 2 with fireplace and private bath. *Pets:*
Inquire first. *Children:* Under 12 not permitted. *Driving instructions:*
The inn is on Route 253, 6 miles east of Boonville.

*Calistoga, California*

## BRANNAN COTTAGE INN

109 Wapoo Avenue, Calistoga, CA 94515. 707-942-4200. *Innkeepers:* Jay and Dottie Richolson. Open all year.

This gingerbread cottage was once one of thirteen cottages that formed the Calistoga Hot Springs Resort. The inn, the sole surviver of the group, has received the Napa Valley Landmark Award for historic preservation. It is surrounded by old-fashioned gardens and has a courtyard scented by lemon trees. The cottage features bleached-oak floors, intricate hand-stenciling, and etched-glass windows. Guest rooms have primitive wood pieces, white wicker, and more formal Victorian furnishing. Each has its own entrance. Guests socialize over sherry or port in the sitting room.

*Accommodations:* 6 rooms with private bath. *Pets, smoking, and children:* Not permitted. *Driving Instructions:* From Route 101, take the Calistoga exit and drive to Calistoga. Go through town and turn left on Wapoo Avenue.

## CULVER'S, A COUNTRY INN

1805 Foothill Boulevard, Calistoga, CA 94515. 707-942-4535. *Innkeepers:* Meg and Tony Wheatley. Open all year except Christmas. In the 1870s, Major John Culver and his wife, Minnie, traveled west from Wisconsin to settle in the Napa Valley. Here, on a hillside with views extending to Mt. Helena, they built their spacious Victorian home. Minnie, an artist who studied under A. G. Wyatt, would enjoy her home today, where bright rooms display the innkeepers' collection of art and antiques. Bare, polished, hardwood floors and white painted walls highlight the dark woods of the antique furnishings.

Each guest room has an unusual quilt covering an antique bed. Upstairs rooms are furnished with Victorian pieces, while downstairs rooms have either Edwardian, Art Deco, or Art Nouveau decor. Days begin with a full breakfast of scones, egg dishes, fruit, and homemade breads. In the early evenings, guests can reconvene by the fire in the parlor to enjoy glasses of sherry and listen to a roll or two on the old player piano. The inn has a sauna and an outdoor swimming pool and patio. Meg and Tony gladly assist guests in planning activities, which could include visits to the hot mineral waters and mudbaths, wine tasting tours, and hot-air ballooning. Winter packages and dinners are available.

*Accommodations:* 6 rooms with shared baths. *Pets and smoking:* Not permitted. *Children:* Under 16 not permitted. *Driving instructions:* Take Route 128 six blocks north of the intersection of Route 29 and turn on Foothill Boulevard.

# FOOTHILL HOUSE

3037 Foothill Boulevard, Calistoga, CA 94515. 707-942-6933. *Innkeepers:* Susan and Michael Clow. Open all year except Christmas.

True to its name, this inn is nestled in foothills, those of the western slopes of the Mayacamas Mountains just north of Calistoga, where quail, hawks, and hummingbirds can be seen quite near the house. Built in 1897 as a farmhouse by one of Calistoga's founding families, Foothill House is now an appealing small inn decorated with country antiques, tiny-print wallpapers, and original works by Wine Country artists.

Susan and Michael are lovers of country inns. Appropriately, each room has a fireplace for winter warmth and a ceiling paddle fan for summer cooling. Rooms are decorated around a color scheme taken from the handmade quilt on each room's four-poster bed. Evergreen Suite has its own terrace and a whirlpool bath, while Redwood Room, named in honor of the towering redwood outside its window, is decorated in rusts and royal blues. Breakfast is served on the terrace, in the Sun Room or, if guests prefer, in their rooms. The Clows host an informative wine-appreciation hour each afternoon; they have added a sundeck.

*Accommodations:* 3 rooms with private bath. *Pets, smoking:* Not permitted. *Driving instructions:* From the center of town, take Route 128 north for 1 1/2 miles to the inn on the left hand side of the road.

## LARKMEAD COUNTRY INN

1103 Larkmead Lane, Calistoga, CA 94515. 707-942-5360. *Innkeeper:* Joan Garbarino. Open January through November.

The Larkmead Country Inn was built in 1918 by the owner of the Larkmead Vineyards and Winery, one of the first wineries in the Napa Valley. The house sits in peace and quiet, surrounded by vineyards and magnolia, cypress, and sycamore trees, behind fieldstone gates.

The inn's Italianate architecture offers broad porches, and flowering vines climb the front portico. In warm months, a Continental breakfast is served on the porch overlooking the grounds. On cooler mornings, breakfast is in the dining room at an antique table set with heirloom china, crystal, and sterling.

The inn is furnished with many antiques set off by Persian carpets. A fine collection of old prints and paintings decorates the walls. Each guest room is named for a Napa Valley wine and overlooks vineyards extending to the distant hills. Guest rooms are air-conditioned and decorated with the innkeeper's antiques. Arriving guests find fresh flowers and a decanter of wine in their rooms.

Many Napa Valley wineries hold summer concerts with such artists as Ella Fitzgerald and Eartha Kitt. The area is ideal for biking on country lanes that pass miles of vineyards. There is glider soaring in Calistoga and hot-air ballooning in Yountville. Calistoga's hot springs, mineral baths, and mud baths attracted visitors long before the first English-speaking settlers arrived.

*Accommodations:* 4 rooms with private bath. *Pets and children:* Not permitted. *Driving Instructions:* Take Route 29 to Larkmead Lane, 4 1/2 miles north of Saint Helena.

## WINE WAY INN

1019 Foothill Boulevard, Calistoga, CA 94515. 707-942-0680. *Innkeepers:* Allen and Dede Good. Open all year.

The Wine Way Inn is a California Craftsman–style house built in 1915 on a highway leading through the wine country. Its guest rooms were named for towns along this "wine way." The Mayacamas Mountains, forming the western slope of Napa Valley, swoop down to the inn's back yard, creating a feeling of country seclusion that is particularly evident when one sits out on the large multilevel deck.

Dede and Allen Good and their little daughter left the hectic pace of southern California to take up a life of innkeeping. After falling in love with the area on a visit in 1980, they bought this inn and furnished it with treasured family antiques. Fresh bouquets of flowers, antique quilts, and decanters of wine add to the appeal of each room. A former buggy-tack room has been transformed into a guest cottage with views of the mountains and valley. Breakfasts of juices, quiches or frittatas, fresh fruits, and coffee are the only meals served.

The inn is with walking distance of town. The Sterling Vineyards, Chateau Montelena, and Schramsberg Vineyards are a ten-minute drive away. Calistoga's spas attract many visitors. The Goods will gladly suggest favorite restaurants and spas for their guests.

*Accommodations:* 6 rooms with private bath (including 1 cottage). *Pets:* Not permitted. *Children:* Under ten not permitted. *Driving Instructions:* Take Route 29 from Napa to Calistoga, where it becomes Foothill Boulevard.

*Cambria, California*

## THE J. PATRICK HOUSE

2990 Burton Drive, Cambria, CA 93428. 805-927-3812. *Innkeeper:* Molly Lynch. Open all year.

The J. Patrick House incorporates a log home with public rooms and a second building containing guest accommodations and a sitting room. Stands of tall pines enhance the inn's peaceful setting. Among Molly's special touches are wood-burning fireplaces, luxurious bath salts, fresh-fruit baskets, and good reading materials in all guest rooms. All rooms are furnished with a variety of antiques and comfortable contemporary pieces, including California willow, oak, brass, and pine furniture. Old-fashioned floral wallpapers, lace curtains, and cedar wainscoting enhance the rooms. Cheeses and local vintage wines are enjoyed by guests at a social hour in the living room. A Continental breakfast starts the day.

Cambria is a village midway between Los Angeles and San Francisco, six miles south of historic Hearst Castle, and close to many other attractions. Big Sur and the central coast vineyards are nearby, and the village has several antique shops, art galleries, boutiques, and good restaurants.

*Accommodations:* 8 rooms with private bath. *Pets, smoking, and children:* Not permitted. *Driving instructions:* The inn is off Route 1.

*Carmel, California*

## COBBLESTONE INN

Junipero and Eighth, Carmel, California. 408-625-5222. Mailing address: P.O. Box 3185, Carmel, CA 93921. *Innkeeper:* Charlie Aldinger. Open all year.

Cobblestone Inn seems to have a little of almost everything one would wish for in an inn. Flower gardens and a cobblestone-enclosed courtyard create a secluded country atmosphere with this busy tourist village by the sea. Country antiques throughout the inn are brightened by colorful quilts and fresh flowers. Each guest room has a cobblestone fireplace for romantic evenings as well as a concealed television and tiny refrigerator stocked with complimentary beverages. At late afternoon teatime, wine, sherry, or tea is served with hors d'oeuvres by the fireside in the parlor. Buffet breakfasts of quiches, omelets, and breakfast pastries can be taken back to the rooms or enjoyed in the parlor or out in the English garden. For guests planning sightseeing jaunts to nearby Point Lobos State Reserve or to Big Sur, the inn staff will supply a well-stocked picnic basket.

*Accommodations:* 24 rooms with private bath. *Pets:* Not permitted. *Driving Instructions:* Take Route 1 to Ocean Avenue, then take Ocean Avenue to Junipero.

# HOLIDAY HOUSE

Camino Real and Seventh Avenue, Carmel, California. Mailing address: P.O. Box 782, Carmel, CA 93921. 408-624-6267. *Innkeepers:* Ruth and Dieter Back. Open all year.

Holiday House, a shingled cottage with dormers and porches poking out in all directions, was built in 1905 as a summer cottage by a Stanford University professor. It was converted to an inn in the 1920s.

The atmosphere here is casual and restful. Guests relax in the living room, in the sun parlor, and, in nice weather, on the sunny terrace overlooking the flower garden. The living room has a rough stone fireplace in which a fire burns on cool mornings and evenings. Guest rooms are furnished in turn-of-the-century decor with many antiques, some original artwork reflecting Carmel's artists' colony, and fresh flowers. We particularly like the guest rooms with sloping ceilings, which add a cozy feeling. Several guest rooms and the living room share a view of the ocean.

This inn is only three blocks from the beach and from the center of town. Thus one can shed the family car on arrival and explore the village on foot, having to contend only with the frequent crowding of other eager tourists. Don't be surprised if some of your fellow guests can recall their visits here more than thirty years ago. One woman came for years as a child accompanied by her grandmother, then returned as an adult recently to be pleasantly surprised that her "old Holiday House" was still the same.

Ruth and Dieter serve a light breakfast each morning; it includes fresh fruit, coffee cake or muffin, choice of cereal, juice, and choice of coffee, tea, or hot chocolate. Often an egg dish is included.

*Accommodations:* 6 rooms, 4 with private bath. *Pets and smoking:* Not permitted. *Children:* Under 13 not permitted. *Driving Instructions:* From Route 1 take the Ocean Avenue exit in Carmel, continue through town to Camino Real, turn left there, and drive one block to the inn.

## HAPPY LANDING INN

Monte Verde, Carmel, California. Mailing address: P.O. Box 2619, Carmel, CA 93921. 408-624-7917. *Innkeepers:* Bob Alberson and Dick Stewart. Open all year.

The Happy Landing Inn consists of two buildings that have six rooms with separate, cottage-like entrances, all around a flower-bedecked courtyard. A lattice gazebo covered with flowering vines and hanging plants is a favorite spot for weddings and receptions. The cottages are painted pink, with slate blue roofs and blue-trimmed windows and doors, which open onto the central garden, with its fish pond and many varieties of flowers, tropical plants, shrubs, and trees. A stone wall encloses the garden.

This collection of Comstock-designed buildings was constructed in 1925 as a private family retreat. Today, each cottage offers guests a stay in a room with a cathedral ceiling, Victorian furniture, and many stained-glass windows throughout. There are two suites with fireplaces as well as one cottage with a fireplace and another with an ocean view. All rooms have color television. Complimentary breakfasts of fruit, pastry, juice, and other beverages are served in the rooms, and each evening a glass of sherry and a good-night "treat" are placed at the bedside. A sitting room contains many antiques.

Happy Landing Inn is just a few steps from Carmel's many boutiques and restaurants, but peaceful enough to enable guests to hear the ocean surf just four blocks away.

*Accommodations:* 7 rooms with private bath. *Pets, smoking, and children:* Not permitted. *Driving Instructions:* Take the Ocean Avenue exit into Carmel. Take Ocean Avenue to Monte Verde, turn right, and go one and a half blocks to the inn.

## SEA VIEW INN

Camino Real, Carmel, California. Mailing address: P.O. Box 4138, Carmel, CA 93921. 408-624-8778. *Innkeepers:* Marshall and Diane Hydorn. Open all year.

The Sea View is a three-story, wood-shingled Victorian house that dates to the first decade of this century. Each room has its own personality, decorated by the Hydorns with a mixture of antique and near-antique pieces in a relaxed and attractive manner. Our favorite is the room above the front porch, with comfy quilts and a private bath. Late in the day, guests may enjoy a glass of sherry together before the living room fireplace. Breakfast is served in the dining area. A private, secluded garden is available where guests may picnic or relax in the sun.

*Accommodations:* 8 rooms, 6 with private bath. *Pets, smoking, and children:* Not permitted. *Driving Instructions:* Take the Ocean Avenue exit into Carmel and to Camino Real; turn left on Camino Real, and drive 5 1/2 blocks to the inn.

## Carmel Valley, California

## ROBLES DEL RIO LODGE

200 Punta del Monte, Carmel Valley, CA 93924. 408-659-2264 or 408-659-3705. *Innkeepers:* The Gurries family. Open all year.

So breathtaking is the coastline of the Monterey Peninsula that many visitors never venture inland. A first-rate reason to do so is a visit to Robles del Rio Lodge, twelve miles from Carmel. The oldest inland lodge in the area still in operation, Robles del Rio was built in 1928 and has been the recipient of two recent renovations. It is a quiet, rustic resort, with both guest rooms and cottages, where guests may explore the surrounding woodland and meadows and use the lodge's tennis court, swimming pool, sauna, and hot tub.

The living room of the main lodge has a cathedral ceiling with exposed beams, a large stone fireplace, and rustic furnishings. The guest rooms have a French countryside look, with modern amenities such as cable television skillfully tucked into an armoire. Many of the cabin rooms have fireplaces, and almost all rooms enjoy a view.

The Ridge restaurant offers regional French cuisine for lunch and dinner to both guests and the public daily except Monday. A Continental breakfast is served to houseguests only; Sunday brunch is served in the courtyard.

*Accommodations:* 31 rooms with private bath. *Pets:* Not permitted. *Driving instructions:* From Route 1, take Carmel Valley Road east 13 miles to Esquiline (just past the village). Turn right, cross 3 small bridges and then take a sharp right onto Los Ositos. Wind up the road to the top and the lodge.

## STONEPINE

150 East Carmel Valley Road, Carmel Valley, CA 93924. 408-659-2245. *Innkeeper:* Dirk Oldenburg. Open all year.

Stonepine, a verdant 330-acre estate with horse pastures and paddocks, is thirteen miles from the Pacific Ocean and was once the private estate of Helen and Henry Russell of the Crocker banking family. A mile-long driveway leads to the sprawling Mediterranean-style manor house surrounded by sixty-year-old stone pines.

There are eight suites in the "Chateau" and an additional four in Paddock House. Also in the Chateau is a 1,200 square-foot master suite that has two dressing rooms, two bathrooms, and two fireplaces. A secret door leads to a tower room. The inn has equestrian facilities, a swimming pool, tennis courts, a gymnasium, and a collection of historic carriages. Formal dinners are served to guests in the dining room or on the porch. Nouvelle American and Continental cuisine highlight the prix fixe dinners. Guests are met at Monterey airport by the inn's Rolls Royce.

*Accommodations:* 12 rooms with private bath. *Pets:* Not permitted. *Children:* Under 12 permitted in Paddock only. *Driving Instructions:* From Route 1, take Carmel Valley Road east approximately 13 miles to the inn.

*Cloverdale, California*

## VINTAGE TOWERS

302 North Main Street, Cloverdale, CA 95425. 707-894-4535. *Innkeepers:* Garrett Hall and Jim Mees. Open February through December.

Vintage Towers is a Queen Anne mansion built around the turn of the century. In 1913, Petaluma architect Brainard Jones added the last two of the three towers and the built-in cabinetwork. The mansion stands on a corner of a tree-lined street behind a rustic stone wall. The lawn is shaded by large flowering mimosas, and the veranda, which has old rockers and a swing, is literally covered with wisteria. Inside the entranceway is the music room, with its piano and rare portable player-piano attachment. Guest suites are tucked into the towers: The Tower Suite has a king-size bed and Victorian wicker furnishings; and the Vintage Suite has a wonderful 8-piece, 1875, walnut bedroom and living room set and a private balcony.

The dining room, with its bay windows and fireplace, is where most guests enjoy their breakfast, although some elect to take theirs out to the rose garden's gazebo, especially on sunny mornings. The library offers more than a thousand volumes plus a fireplace.

*Accommodations:* 7 rooms, 5 with private bath. *Pets:* Not permitted. *Children:* Under 10 not permitted. *Driving Instructions:* The inn is one block east of U.S. 101, at the corner of Third and North Main

*Columbia, California*

## CITY HOTEL

Main Street, Columbia, California. Mailing address: P.O. Box 1870, Columbia, CA 95310. 209-532-1479. *Innkeeper:* Tom Bender. Open all year.

In 1856, in the midst of the gold fever that had followed the discovery of gold in Columbia, George Morgan began construction of the hotel that remains a monument to that era. His two-story brick hotel was known as the What Cheer House until 1984 when it was renamed the City Hotel. In 1974, the building was completely restored with the help of state and federal funds. It now serves as a gracious Victorian hotel partially staffed by students receiving training in hospitality management at Columbia Junior College.

The brick building with its wood and iron balconies and boardwalk only hints at the gracious interior. Public rooms have been restored in the style (although not the opulence) of the Victorian era. Guest rooms include those with private balconies overlooking the tree-lined Main Street, parlor rooms that open directly onto the main sitting parlor, and the smaller but still ornately furnished hall rooms. Each has its own toilet and marble sink. However, true to the Gold Rush era, bathing involves a walk down the hall to the shower. Included in the room rate is a Continental breakfast. At dinner, cooking is done under the supervision of a French chef, and the meals are haute cuisine.

*Accommodations:* 9 rooms with sink and toilet, sharing hall bath. *Pets:* Not permitted. *Smoking:* Restricted. *Driving Instructions:* Columbia State Park is off Route 49. Main Street is closed to traffic during the day, but the hotel may be approached from a side street.

## FALLON HOTEL

Washington Street, Columbia, California. Mailing address: P.O. Box 1870, Columbia, CA 95310. 209-532-1470. *Innkeeper:* Tom Bender. Open all year; weekends only, November, January, and February.

This inn is an 1857 Victorian hotel with an adjacent theater and ice cream parlor. It is a part of the Columbia Historic Park. The hotel has an abundance of fans, feathers, paisley prints, and properly fussy furniture, along with Oriental and floral wallpapers. Many of the original furnishings and decorative pieces have been retained.

Guest accommodations include antique furnishings, and several rooms have private balconies. All rooms have half baths, but showers are located in separate hall bath rooms. Guests are provided with robes, slippers, and toiletries for the hallway trip. The hotel provides a Continental breakfast.

*Accommodations:* 13 rooms with half-baths, 1 with full bath. *Pets:* Not permitted. *Smoking:* Permitted in parlor only. *Driving Instructions:* From Sonora, take Route 49 north 2 miles to the fork in the road. Take the right fork and drive 2 miles to Columbia. The hotel is the first brick building on the right.

## NEW DAVENPORT BED AND BREAKFAST

31 Davenport Avenue, Box J, Davenport, CA 95017. 408-425-1818.
*Innkeepers:* Bruce and Marcia McDougal. Open all year.

This bed-and-breakfast inn stands next to the New Davenport Cash Store on the coast highway northwest of Santa Cruz. Both the store and the inn are the creations of artists Marcia and Bruce McDougal, who, after they had founded the nearby Big Creek Ranch, a landmark pottery school, wanted a retail outlet for the school's crafts. They bought the highway site and, after researching early Gold County California architecture, built the store and studio. Later the McDougals added the restaurant and inn.

The building that houses the inn was originally a bathhouse at the turn of the century, but its four guest rooms are furnished today with antique iron beds, old-fashioned oaken dressers, and a treasure trove of local crafts and folkware collected by Bruce and Marcia on their travels. There are eight more rooms above the store, each opening onto an outside deck with views of the surf and rocky coast just across the highway. These rooms contain a blend of antiques and ethnic art objects.

The restaurant is a family affair with McDougal offspring and their spouses baking breads and pastries, stirring soups, and otherwise cooking up fresh fare. The same building also houses the Cash Store, a shop filled with a wide variety of pottery, rugs, jewelry, and folk art from around the world.

*Accommodations:* 12 rooms with private bath. *Pets:* Not permitted. *Smoking:* Restricted. *Children:* One room only. *Driving Instructions:* Davenport is 9 miles northwest of Santa Cruz on Route 1, halfway between San Francisco and Carmel.

## ROCK HAUS BED AND BREAKFAST INN

410 Fifteenth Street, Del Mar, CA 92014. 619-481-3764. *Innkeeper:* Doris Holmes. Open all year.

Just up the hill from the old seaside village of Del Mar, with its little shops and restaurants, is a historic landmark, the Rock Haus Bed and Breakfast Inn. Built in 1910 as a private home in the California-bungalow style, the sturdy house was restored in the 1980s. On a hill just three blocks from the ocean, the inn offers guests a chance both to see and to hear the sea.

One room, Whale Watch, contains whaling artifacts and has a bed set high enough to enable guests to see whales during their migration and to enjoy spectacular sunsets. Huntsman's Room is done in rich greens and red with white accents. It has fox-hunting prints and decoys set on the mantel over the working fireplace. Each of the other rooms has its own special appeal—field flowers painted on a rescued armoire, ocean views, or a whispering Torrey pine outside a French window. The hearth in the living room is a favorite gathering spot on cool evenings or foggy mornings. A glassed-in veranda with sea views is the setting for breakfasts and for refreshments at the end of the day.

*Accommodations:* 10 rooms, 4 with private bath. *Pets, smoking, and children:* Not permitted. *Driving Instructions:* From San Diego take I-5 north to Via de la Valle. Turn left onto Via de la Valle, left again onto Jimmy Durante Boulevard, and a third time onto Fifteenth Street; then go one more block to the inn.

*East Brother Island, California*

## EAST BROTHER LIGHT STATION

East Brother Island, California. Mailing address: 117 Park Place, Point Richmond, CA 94801. 415-233-2385. *Innkeepers:* Linda and Leigh Hurley. Open all year.

East Brother Island is one of four islands marking the straits separating San Francisco and San Pablo Bay. The Light Station was constructed in 1873–74, and it is the oldest one still in operation. The former Victorian living quarters now have pastel colors outlined by crisp white gingerbread trim. Its guest rooms are furnished with period antiques and wall coverings, while its parlor has a wood-burning stove. Breakfast and lavish five-course, California-style French dinners are served in the antique-furnished dining room. Guests should be aware that water is in short supply, and showers are normally available only by special arrangement. The Light Station is booked almost a year in advance, so reserve early.

*Accommodations:* 4 rooms, 2 with private bath. *Pets:* Not permitted. *Children:* By prior arrangement only. *Driving Instructions:* The inn provides boat transportation from Point San Pablo Yacht Harbor, about 10 miles north of Berkeley.

*Elk, California*

## ELK COVE INN

P.O. Box 367, Elk, CA 95432. 707-877-3321. *Innkeeper:* Hildrun-Uta Triebess. Open all year.

Elk Cove Inn, a Victorian house high on a bluff overlooking the rocky coast and the ever-changing ocean, looks European, surrounded as it is by old-fashioned flower gardens. A red rose twists its way up the porch post, and flower-filled window boxes line the porch roof. A path winds down to the driftwood-strewn, secluded beaches.

The inn was built in 1883 by one of the area's largest lumber companies for its superintendent. In 1967 innkeeper Hildrun-Uta Triebess fell in love with the place and spent months repairing, repainting, and redecorating. The inn has dining rooms, a big living room with fireplace, and the innkeeper's living quarters. A remodeled cabin behind the main house has bedrooms with Victorian wallpapers and ocean views, as does the hand-painted-tile bathroom. Two rooms have high, beamed ceilings, skylights, free-standing Victorian fireplaces, 8-foot bay windows, and wainscoting.

Hildrun-Uta, who spent her childhood in Germany, is an excellent cook whose specialties are German and French cuisine. Her breakfasts include specialties such as Eierkuchen (German souflée egg cakes served with rasberry and plum sauce) and orange soufflé omelets.

*Accommodations:* 7 rooms with private bath. *Pets, smoking, and children:* Not permitted. *Driving Instructions:* The inn is 4 1/2 hours up the coast from San Francisco on Route 1. The drive is only 3 1/2 hours if you take Route 101 from San Francisco to Cloverdale, then Route 128 to the coast at Route 1, then left (south), 5 miles to Elk.

## HARBOR HOUSE

> 5600 Coast Highway 1, Elk, California. Mailing address: Box 369, Elk, CA 95432. 707-877-3203. *Innkeepers:* Helen and Dean Turner. Open all year.

Harbor House is a redwood estate built in the early 1900s to lodge visiting lumber-company executives from the East. The inn has fine detailing everywhere; its crowning glory is a living room with vaulted, beamed ceiling, a large fireplace, and doorways and walls covered with redwood panels still perfectly preserved by a layer of beeswax that was hand-rubbed into it when the inn was built. Workmen painstakingly carved, fitted, and rubbed each piece.

The furnishings and decor throughout are of a splendor in keeping with the house. The innkeeper has re-created an Edwardian atmosphere with period antiques, overstuffed chairs, and well-stocked bookcases. There is a fine collection of old photographs of turn-of-the-century logging operations, showing the tramways and big lumber-carrying schooners. The inn has six guest rooms in the main house and four cottages (each a single unit) perched on the bluffs next to the inn. The cottages, furnished with antiques and Franklin stoves on brick hearths, have views of the ocean, the water-eroded rock formations, and the private beach below. The inn's guest rooms have full-size fireplaces, antique furnishings, delicate floral wallpapers, and electric blankets on the king- and queen-size beds.

Meals are served in traditional country-inn style with one menu, plenty of food, and a crackling fire in the fireplace. Not so traditional is the breathtaking view of the rugged coast from the windows. Breakfasts and dinners are served to the public with a day's advance reservation. Some of the inn's specialties are marinated ling cod, champagne chicken, and petrale sole Florentine in pastry. Two favorite desserts are mocha toffee pie and custard and fresh fruit in puffs. Everything here is fresh and made from scratch — from the soups to the hot, fragrant breads and rolls. The wine list includes the best from the local wineries. The inn also serves a variety of beers and ales, but no hard liquor.

*Accommodations:* 10 rooms with private bath. *Pets:* Not permitted. *Smoking:* Restricted. *Children:* Under 16 not permitted. *Driving Instructions:* Three hours from San Francisco on Route 101 to Cloverdale. From Cloverdale take Route 128 to Coast Highway, Route 1. Harbor House is 6 miles to the south in Elk.

## CARTER HOUSE INN

1033 Third Street, Eureka, CA 95501. 707-445-1390. *Innkeepers:* Mark and Christi Carter. Open all year.

In 1884, Samuel and Joseph Newsome designed and built an unusual many-gabled Victorian house for the Murphy family in San Francisco. Although the house was totally destroyed in the 1906 earthquake, its plans were preserved. Several years ago, Mark Carter decided to re-create the house as a bed-and-breakfast inn almost 300 miles to the north, in Eureka.

True to the period, Mark's construction included a clear redwood exterior and polished oak and redwood with. Trims and moldings were handmade, and two brick chimneys were built to heights of over 50 feet. The Victorian decor is enhanced by marble and hardwood floors, Oriental carpeting, potted plants, and fresh-cut flowers. On arrival, guests are offered wine and hors d'oeuvres. Cookies, tea, and cordials are set out as bedtime treats, and in the morning Mark serves his 4-course breakfast. Twelve restaurants are with walking distance.

*Accommodations:* 7 rooms, 4 with private bath. *Pets and smoking:* Not permitted. *Children:* Under 10 not permitted. *Driving Instructions:* The inn is on the corner of Third and L streets, 2 blocks from the Marina at the gateway to Old Town.

## HOTEL CARTER

301 L Street, Eureka, CA 95501. 707-445-1390. *Innkeepers:* Mark and Christi Carter. Open all year.

A replica of one of Eureka's historic landmarks — the nineteenth-century Old Town Cairo Hotel — the Hotel Carter in its present incarnation has views of Humboldt Bay and offers dining and lodging in an European-style setting. Guest rooms are furnished with antique pine and decorated with original artwork. Several rooms have working fireplaces, and some baths have Jacuzzis.

Wine and hors d'oeuvres are served in the early evening beside a fire in the lobby. Breakfasts — voted the best in California by *California Magazine,* — and dinners are served to overnight guests and the public by reservation only. The fresh, innovative dinner menu changes seasonally. The menu includes such items as red pepper bisque with yellow pepper cream and a mixed grill of local salmon, halibut, mussels, clams, and crayfish bathed in an avocado basil sauce. Meals are served in a candlelit setting.

*Accommodations:* 20 rooms with private baths. *Pets:* Not permitted. *Smoking:* In lobby only. *Driving Instructions:* From southbound Route 101, turn right on L Street; from the north, turn left on L Street.

*Ferndale, California*

## THE GINGERBREAD MANSION

400 Berding Street, Ferndale, CA 95536. 707-786-4000. *Innkeepers:* Wendy Hatfield and Ken Torbert. Open all year.

Originally built in 1898 as a residence for a physician, the Gingerbread Mansion has served the Victorian village of Ferndale, among other ways, as a hospital and an American Legion hall. In 1983 this Victorian fantasy was restored and opened as a bed-and-breakfast inn. With its gingerbread trim painted in yellow and peach tones, and surrounded by a colorful English garden, the turreted, carved, and steeply gabled structure has become one of northern California's most photographed buildings.

Within, the Gingerbread Mansion has been restored to its late-nineteenth-century elegance. The large guest rooms, including three with a wood-burning stoves, are filled with antiques. The bathrooms are as unique as the rest of the house—Gingerbread and Fountain suites each have two claw-footed tubs! A homemade Continental breakfast is served downstairs, and afternoon tea and cake are set out in one of the four spacious parlors. Wendy and Ken provide such special "extras" as rainboots and umbrellas, bathrobes, hand-dipped chocolates by the bedside, and even bicycles painted to match the colorful house.

*Accommodations:* 9 rooms with private bath. *Pets and smoking:* Not permitted. *Children:* Under 10 not permitted. *Driving Instructions:* From Eureka, take Route 101 south 20 miles to the Ferndale Exit. Drive 5 miles to Main Street, turn left at the Bank of America, and go one block farther.

## SHAW HOUSE INN

703 Main Street, Ferndale, California. Mailing address: Box 1125, Ferndale, CA 95536. 707-786-9958. *Innkeepers:* Ken and Norma Bessingpas. Open all year.

Shaw House, listed in the National Register of Historic Places, was built in 1854 by Seth Louis Shaw, the founder of the town of Ferndale. Its steep center gable is flanked by a pair of similarly proportioned dormers and, below, by twin porches. These architectural elements are typical of a classic Carpenter Gothic home of the period. Shaw House is surrounded by gardens, stately trees, and a creek.

The rooms with are filled with art, antiques, books, and memorabilia. There is a large library with a fireplace. Guest rooms at Shaw House, tucked under the gables or into bay windows, feature woodwork, shuttered windows, carpeting, and antique furnishings. The Honeymoon Suite has the original Shaw honeymoon bed from a century ago. Rooms have fresh-flower arrangements.

Ferndale is an historic California village where the descendants of early settlers still operate dairy or sheep farms. There are outstanding craft and art galleries, blacksmith shops, and an excellent museum of local history, as well as wilderness hiking trails in nearby Russ Park.

*Accommodations:* 6 rooms, 1 with half bath, 2 with private bath. *Pets, smoking, and children:* Not permitted. *Driving Instructions:* Take the Fernbridge–Ferndale off-ramp from Route 101. Ferndale is about 5 miles west of Fernbridge.

## COLONIAL INN

533 East Fir Street, Fort Bragg, California. Mailing address: P.O. Box 565, Fort Bragg, CA 95437. 707-964-9979. *Innkeepers:* Donald and Catherine Markham. Open all year except three weeks in October and two weeks in the spring.

Colonial Inn, in a quiet residential section of Fort Bragg, was built as a private home in the early 1900s and became a guest house in 1945. The grounds are most pleasant, with a big lawn and tall palms.

The Markhams provide eight comfortable guest rooms with television and private bath. Two have wood-burning fireplaces, and wood is supplied for them. All the rooms at the inn are carpeted, and furnishings are early California. The Markhams love plants, which can be found just about everywhere. Food is not served at the Colonial, but there are a number of good restaurants nearby. The Skunk Railroad Depot is six blocks from the inn.

The innkeepers at the Colonial Inn have made it a fine place to use as a home base while exploring the area. The Markhams can steer you to wild blackberry and huckleberry patches in season and know (but may not tell) the best spots to hunt mushrooms. Beachcombing is great any time of the year, and tennis courts are close by.

*Accommodations:* 8 rooms with private bath. *Pets:* Not permitted. *Smoking:* Restricted. *Driving Instructions:* The inn is 4 blocks east of Route 1.

# COUNTRY INN

632 North Main Street, Fort Bragg, CA 95437. 707-964-3737. *Innkeepers:* Don and Helen Miller. Open all year.

Fort Bragg developed in the last quarter of the nineteenth century as a center for the rapidly expanding redwood lumber industry. Indeed, the first recorded deed transaction involving the house now known as the Country Inn was in 1893, when one L. A. Moody acquired the original building for $500 from the Union Lumber Company.

In restoring their place, the innkeepers retained the redwood moldings, banisters, and wainscoting and have added floral-print wall coverings and replicas of period lighting fixtures. There is a skylighted sitting room with a bricked-back potbellied stove and a redwood sun deck. One of the popular guest rooms is tucked into the attic eaves. Two rooms have fireplaces.

Innkeeper Helen Miller prepares fresh-baked fruit breads and muffins for the complimentary Continental breakfast. Don Miller is an artist, designer, sculptor, and photographer, and several examples of his work are on display at the inn. The Skunk Railroad Depot, shops, restaurants, and Glass Beach, with its rounded bits of glass from a turn-of-the-century brewery, are all within a few blocks.

*Accommodations:* 8 rooms with private bath. *Pets, smoking, and children:* Not permitted. *Driving Instructions:* Take Route 1 to Fort Bragg, where it becomes North Main Street.

## PUDDING CREEK INN

700 North Main Street, Fort Bragg, CA 95437. 707-964-9529. *Innkeepers:* Marilyn and Eugene Gundersen. Open all year except January.

In the late 1880s a Russian count fell into disfavor with the tsar and fled to Fort Bragg, bringing many of the royal family's jewels with him—or so it is rumored. The count built a series of houses, including the two that make up the Pudding Creek Inn.

Named for the little creek that runs from the nearby redwood forests to the sea, the inn is the brainchild of former teachers Marilyn and Gene Gundersen. They transformed the two Victorian houses into a country inn with a garden courtyard planted in begonias, fuchsias, and ferns. The guest rooms are decorated in a Victorian or country-antique manner. Each room's name conveys its special charms: The Count's Room is all cranberry velvets, with a stone fireplace and its original inlaid redwood paneling; Buttercup is done in cheery yellows and green that set off a bed made of bird's-eye maple. A breakfast of homemade coffee cakes, fresh fruit, and an egg dish such as eggs Benedict. The Country Store, housed in the inn, is a nice place to browse for old-fashioned gifts. The inn is two blocks from the beach. Skunk Train Depot is nearby.

*Accommodations:* 10 rooms with private bath. *Pets and smoking:* Not permitted. *Children:* Under 10 not permitted. *Driving Instructions:* Route 1 becomes Main Street in Fort Bragg. The inn is at the north end of town.

## BENBOW INN

445 Lake Benbow Drive, Garberville, CA 95440. 707-923-2124. *Innkeepers:* Chuck and Patsy Watts. Open mid-April through November and three weeks in December.

Close your eyes as you pull into the Benbow Inn and you will open them to find that you have arrived at what appears to be an English Tudor mansion surrounded by conifers. In April the inn's 1,100 tulips will greet you in colorful profusion, but any season brings its share of beauty to the English gardens. The stately inn at the edge of Benbow Lake also has an adjacent nine-hole golf course and tennis courts. Built in 1926 by nine members of the Benbow family, it was designed by Albert Farr, noted for his outstanding Tudor creations. Perhaps his most romantic work was Wolf House, in Glen Ellen, built for the author Jack London, which was destroyed by fire shortly before the writer was to move in. Happily, the Benbow Inn lives on.

From the moment you enter the lobby, you know you are in one of the country's more special inns. Its collection of fine antiques, many of museum quality, includes an extensive sampling of early clocks. The walls are hung with many antique (and some reproduction) pictures, floors are covered with Oriental rugs, and *objets d'art* fascinate and enchant the viewer. Guest rooms carry out the antique theme with selections of drapes, pillow shams, and dust ruffles in matching antique prints. Some rooms have fireplaces; others have color television.

Dining at the Benbow is an event at any time of the day. Breakfasts offer a number of American standards, but the omelets with several fillings and topped with mornay sauce are the featured specialty. The brunch menu, available Sunday from 10:00 to 1:30, features several elegant presentations of eggs, quiche, crepes, and apple blintzes. The evening menu is about evenly divided between Continental specialties — such as white Wisconsin veal in Marsala and piccata variations — and seafood creations including scallops St. Jacques and prawns Eric. Selections from the broiler include tournedos, New York steaks, and ribeye. A complete vegetarian meal is generally available. Chocolate-mousse pie leads the dessert list in popularity.

*Accommodations:* 55 rooms with private bath. *Pets:* Not permitted. *Driving Instructions:* The inn is 200 miles north of San Francisco and 2 miles south of Garberville, on Route 101.

## Georgetown, California

## HISTORIC AMERICAN RIVER INN

Main at Orleans Street, Georgetown, California. Mailing address: P.O. Box 43, Georgetown, CA 95634. 916-333-4499. *Innkeepers:* Will and Maria Collin and Carol Lamonte. Open all year.

The American River Inn was originally built in 1853 as The American Hotel—a boardinghouse for gold miners from surrounding mining camps—and was later a stagecoach stop. The Mother Lode of the Woodside Mine still runs beneath the hotel, which burned in 1899 and was immediately rebuilt. When Maria and Will purchased the the property, they polished floors, papered the walls with flower prints, and decorated the rooms with Victorian country antiques. Scrolly iron and brass beds in the guest rooms have down comforters and antique quilts. Lace curtains add to the look, as do old-fashioned light fixtures. The fireside in the parlor is the setting for evening tastings of wines from some of the area's nine vineyards. Breakfast is served by the fireplace in the dining room or, on sunny days, out on the patio overlooking Victorian-style gardens. The grounds include a mountain pool, a Jacuzzi, a dove aviary, as well as the the Queen Anne House. The nearby Sierra Nevada foothills afford miles of hiking trails, and guests may try their hand at white-water rafting on the American River.

*Accommodations:* 18 rooms and 7 suites, 15 with private bath. *Pets:* Not permitted. *Children:* Under 9 not permitted. *Driving Instructions:* From Auburn, I-80 and exit at Route 49 south to Route 193. From Placerville, I-50 and exit at Route 49 north to Route 193.

## Geyserville, California

### HOPE-MERRILL HOUSE

21253 Geyserville Avenue, Geyserville, California. Mailing address: P.O. Box 42, Geyserville, CA 95441. 707-857-3356. *Innkeepers:* Rosalie and Bob Hope. Open all year.

The Hope-Merrill House was built sometime between 1870 and 1885 by J. P. Merrill, one of Geyserville's early pioneers. The town derived its name from the geysers here at one of the largest geothermal fields in the world.

The house, an Eastlake stick-style Victorian, is a tribute to Bob and Rosalie Hope's skills as meticulous restorers. They did careful research on wallpapers of the period and decorated the guest rooms, parlor, and dining room with museum hand-reproduced papers and friezes. The original lighting fixtures, quarter-sawn oak doors and woodwork, and an unusual cast-iron fireplace mantel painted to resemble Italian marble are set off by the rich, deep colors of these wall coverings.

The parlor with its Eastlake furniture overlooks rolling hills, vineyards, and Geyser Peak. It is difficult to choose a favorite among the guest rooms here. Peacock Room, named for the peacock frieze that borders William Morris paper, has its own fireplace and Jacuzzi for two. Gothic Room also has a double tub and an airy skylight.

Full country breakfasts are served family style in the dining room. In back is a sun parlor, where guests can relax and enjoy a glass of wine, and a heated swimming pool.

*Accommodations:* 7 rooms with private bath. *Pets and smoking:* Not permitted. *Children:* Inquire first. *Driving Instructions:* From San Francisco, take U.S. 101 73 miles north to the Geyserville exit. Take Geyserville Avenue through town. The inn is on the west side of the road.

# HOPE-MERRILL HOUSE

21253 Geyserville Avenue, Geyserville, California. Mailing address: P.O. Box 42, Geyserville, CA 95441. 707-857-3356. *Innkeepers:* Rosalie and Bob Hope. Open all year.

The Hope-Merrill House was built sometime between 1870 and 1885 by J. P. Merrill, one of Geyserville's early pioneers. The town derived its name from the geysers here at one of the largest geothermal fields in the world.

The house, an Eastlake stick-style Victorian, is a tribute to Bob and Rosalie Hope's skills as meticulous restorers. They did careful research on wallpapers of the period and decorated the guest rooms, parlor, and dining room with museum hand-reproduced papers and friezes. The original lighting fixtures, quarter-sawn oak doors and woodwork, and an unusual cast-iron fireplace mantel painted to resemble Italian marble are set off by the rich, deep colors of these wall coverings.

The parlor with its Eastlake furniture overlooks rolling hills, vineyards, and Geyser Peak. It is difficult to choose a favorite among the guest rooms here. Peacock Room, named for the peacock frieze that borders William Morris paper, has its own fireplace and Jacuzzi for two. Gothic Room also has a double tub and an airy skylight.

Full country breakfasts are served family style in the dining room. In back is a sun parlor, where guests can relax and enjoy a glass of wine, and a swimming pool.

*Accommodations:* 5 rooms with private bath. *Pets:* Not permitted. *Children:* Inquire first. *Driving Instructions:* From San Francisco, take U.S. 101 73 miles north to the Geyserville exit. Take Geyserville Avenue through town. The inn is on the west side of the road.

## Glen Ellen, California

### BELTANE RANCH

11775 Sonoma Highway, Glen Ellen, California. Mailing address: P.O. Box 395, Glen Ellen, CA 95442. 707-996-6501. *Innkeeper:* Rosemary Wood. Open all year except January.

Beltane Ranch was built in 1892 for an apparently quite successful madame who earned her riches in San Francisco and retired to this beautiful hillside property overlooking the Sonoma Valley. The ranch has been in innkeeper Rosemary Woods' family for over fifty years. Today it offers simple, unpretentious, but comfortable overnight accommodations in what was formerly the ranch bunkhouse.

Porches offer vistas of the ivy-covered shade trees and lush gardens, as well as of the surrounding vineyards, including the ranch's own grapes, from which the Beltane Chardonnay is bottled by the nearby Kenwood Winery. The three upstairs guest rooms, two of which have their own sitting rooms, are accessible from an outside stairway. On warmer mornings, breakfast is served out on the porch, and in the cooler months, by the fireside downstairs. There are walking trails and a tennis court. Nicest of all, Beltane has a sense of the authentic.

*Accommodations:* 4 rooms with private bath. *Pets:* Not permitted. *Children:* Over 5, by prior arrangement. *Smoking:* Restricted. *Driving:* The ranch is 8 miles north of Sonoma on Route 12.

## Grass Valley, California

# ANNIE HORAN'S BED & BREAKFAST

415 West Main Street, Grass Valley, CA 95945. 916-272-2418. *Innkeepers:* Pat and Tom Kiddy. Open all year.

Annie Horan's father built this sumptious Victorian house with money earned from investing in local gold mines during the mid-nineteenth century. Annie inherited the home in 1900 and opened it as a boarding house and retreat for the Catholic Church, remaining its innkeeper until her death in 1954. Thanks to her, most of the building's architectural features remain little changed, and today, the present owner-innkeepers are continuing that tradition, maintaining an atmosphere authentic to the Boom-Town days of Grass Valley.

The parlor has Queen Anne furnishings, as does the dining room, where the morning meal is served. On warm, sunny days, breakfast is also served outside on the deck. The early-evening social hour includes good conversation accompanied by California cheeses, juices, and herbal teas. Tom is a private pilot and will pick up fellow pilots at the Grass Valley airport.

*Accommodations:* 4 rooms with private bath. *Pets and smoking:* Not permitted. *Driving instructions:* From I-80, take the Grass Valley Route 49; continue north 16 miles to Grass Valley. Take the South Auburn exit; continue west on Main.

## THE HOLBROOKE HOTEL

212 West Main, Grass Valley, CA 95945. 916-273-1353. *Manager:* Judy Rosas. Open all year.

Gold was discovered in Grass Valley when a man chasing his cow kicked a rock that turned out to be gold quartz. Soon after, in 1851, pioneer Clara Smith built the Golden Gate Saloon. In 1855 a disastrous fire swept the town, destroying almost all the buildings in an hour and a half. The saloon was rebuilt, this time out of fieldstone faced with brick, the status symbol of the day. In 1862 the Exchange Hotel was built next door, and somewhere along the way the two were incorporated into the Holbrooke Hotel. The hotel has undergone a restoration under the ownership of local businessmen who banded together to save the historic structure. Its seventeen guest rooms are furnished with period antiques including brass beds, some with canopies, and armoires that hide television sets. Six rooms open onto private verandas, and two rooms have working fireplaces. The Golden Gate Saloon, in continuous operation since Clara's time, is the oldest operating saloon in the state. Today, its old back bar, ceiling fans, and brass and oak furnishings create a nostalgic atmosphere of the Old West.

*Accommodations:* 17 rooms with private bath. *Pets:* Not permitted. *Children:* Under 12 not permitted. *Driving Instructions:* From I-80 take Route 49 or Route 20 to Grass Valley. The inn is on Main Street between Church and Mill streets.

## MURPHY'S INN

318 Neal Street, Grass Valley, CA 95945. 916-273-6873. *Innkeeper:* Marc and Rose Murphy. Open all year.

This symmetrical Victorian house is one of the most handsome in the California gold country and one of the most frequently photographed. It was built in 1866 on the estate of one of the region's gold barons, Edward Coleman, owner of the Idaho and North Star mines. The house has been kept in such tip-top condition over the years that it is difficult to distinguish photographs taken of it today from those taken many years ago. The only obvious changes are in the size of the majestic sequoia beside the house and the spa with a large sundeck the Murphys have added.

The preservation of a Victorian look has been accomplished inside as well. Almost all of the interior here is original, including four marble-and-tile fireplaces and the gas-burning chandeliers. The parlor has a working fireplace that is faced with marble and has a cherry-wood mantel with a matching built-in desk and bookshelf alongside. The rooms are furnished with period antiques, lace curtains, and floral wallpapers. A full breakfast is the only meal served.

*Accommodations:* 8 rooms, 6 with private bath. *Pets and smoking:* Not permitted. *Children:* Restricted. *Driving Instructions:* Take I-80 to Auburn, then Route 49 to the Colfax exit; left at the stop sign and left on Neal Street.

## OLD MILANO HOTEL

38300 Highway 1, Gualala, CA 95445. 707-884-3256. *Innkeeper:* Leslie Linscheid. Open all year.

The Old Milano Hotel is in a splendid location: on a cliff overlooking the ocean and the rugged Pacific coastline where the surf pounds cliffs and boulders smooth.

The hotel is listed in the National Register of Historic Places. It was built in 1905 by the Lucchinetti family as a saloon to serve the old stage road and the railroad, which clung to the edges of the cliffs. Cedar trees the Lucchinettis planted as a windbreak are still here, creating an oasis of calm around the hotel. Flowers grow here in colorful profusion.

Most guest rooms overlook the cove below and its wave-pounded Castle Rock. The rooms have been restored with Victorian furnishings. Downstairs are the Wine Parlor, with its stone fireplace, and the Music Room, with its collection of art books. The Lucchinetti family's original rooms are now The Suite, which includes a little sitting room looking out to sea, a bedroom, and a private bath. Also available is the Passion Vine Cottage, in the flower garden, covered with its namesake. The Caboose, a dream come true for railroad buffs, even has an observation cupola. Along with its scenery, gardens, fresh sea air, and romantic rooms, the Old Milano Hotel offers a hot tub.

A full breakfast including home-baked breads is offered to guests as breakfast in bed, on the sunny, plant-filled loggia, or by the parlor fireplace. Evening meals, featuring fresh seasonal dishes, are served Wednesday through Sunday by reservation only.

*Accommodations:* 9 rooms, 3 with private bath. *Pets and children:* Not permitted. *Smoking:* Restricted. *Driving Instructions:* The inn is a mile north of Gualala on the ocean side of Route 1.

## SAINT ORRES

36601 Highway One, Gualala, California. Mailing address: P.O. Box 523, Gualala, CA 95445. 707-884-3303. *Innkeeper:* Gwynne Nelson. Open all year.

Saint Orres, north of Gualala, is distinguished by twin Russian-style towers that rise more than 50 feet to their gleaming copper octagonal roofs. Each tower has an array of many-paned windows rising in ranks to a single row of stained-glass windows just below the copper crown.

The walls of the rooms are faced with redwood carefully matched to form repeating designs. Upstairs are eight guest rooms, which share three baths labeled "His," "Hers," and "Ours." Quilts are patchwork. Nearby are other choices: Three cottages behind the inn and seven at creekside. Many feature wood-burning stoves or fireplaces, skylights, and ocean views from their sundecks. The creekside cottages have access to a sauna and hot tub.

The *prix-fixé* menu features mainly Continental cuisine, with a fresh-fish entrée and a daily chef's special. Reservations are recommended.

*Accommodations:* 8 rooms sharing baths, 10 cottages. *Pets:* Not permitted. *Children:* In cottages only. *Driving Instructions:* The inn is 2 miles north of Gualala, on Route 1.

*Guerneville, California*

## RIDENHOUR RANCH HOUSE INN

12850 River Road, Guerneville, CA 95446. 707-887-1033. *Inn-keepers:* Diane and Fritz Rechberger. Open all year.

The Ridenhour family came from Missouri to California in 1850 and, in 1856, began to farm 940 acres of land on both sides of the Russian River. Their son, Louis, built a one-and-a-half–story ranch house on 2 1/4 acres of land, and today the home receives guests on a spot just 500 yards east of the historic Korbel Champagne Cellars.

The sturdy eleven-room country house was built of heart redwood in a period of Western history when wood was plentiful. It has a big country kitchen, a formal dining room, and a living room. Chef-owner Rick Jewell prepares luncheons and dinners by special arrangement.

Each guest room is decorated individually with brass-and-iron beds set off by country quilts, English and American country antiques, and fresh flowers or potted plants.

The inn's informally landscaped grounds offer paths that meander under redwood and oak trees. Secluded river beaches are a short stroll away, and a hot tub is available. The inn's orchards supply apples, persimmons, plums, pears, and figs.

*Accommodations:* 8 rooms, 5 with private bath. *Pets and smoking:* Not permitted. *Children:* Under 10 not permitted. *Driving Instructions:* The inn is 12 miles west of Route 101, on River Road.

## Half Moon Bay, California

### OLD THYME INN

779 Main Street, Half Moon Bay, CA 94019. 415-726-1616. *Innkeepers:* Simon and Anne Lowings. Open all year.

This family-run Queen Anne Victorian inn is with walking distance of Half Moon Bay's shops and seafood restaurants. It is decorated with antiques of the period. Each guest room is named for a particular herbal theme. Mint Room and Thyme Room have working fireplaces, and the latter has a whirlpool bath and canopy bed, while Mint offers glimpses of the ocean. The garden suite has a private entrance through the herb garden and includes a whirlpool tub for two, a four-poster bed, a fireplace, a television, and a VCR with tapes. Simon is the breakfast chef—specialties include scones, tortes, and fruit soups. Simon and Anne are glad to help guests with restaurant choices.

*Accommodations:* 6 rooms, 5 with private bath. *Pets:* Inquire. *Smoking:* Not permitted. *Children:* Permitted (over 6) on weekdays only. *Driving Instructions:* Take Route 1 into Half Moon Bay; turn east on Kelly Street and then south on Main Street.

### SAN BENITO HOTEL

356 Main Street, Half Moon Bay, CA 94019. 415-726-3425. *Innkeeper:* Carol Mickelsen. Open all year.

Behind the façade of the San Benito Hotel lies an inn with a European flavor. Carol trained in France with Roger Verge at the restaurant Moulin de Mougins, near Nice, and with Giuliano Bugialli in Florence, Ita-

ly. She brought back from France a number of European decorative accessories that have been installed in the hotel. Steps off the redwood deck out back lead to the herb and vegetable gardens that supply some of the fresh produce. A large glass-walled deck off the upper hall provides a sunny spot from which to watch the ocean. The lawn is often set up for croquet or badminton.

Guest rooms feature brass beds, antique lighting fixtures, old trunks, paintings, and fresh flowers. Rooms on the garden side are somewhat more elaborate and are priced higher. A Continental breakfast, served in the dining room or on the sun deck, is included. A three-course, prix fixé dinner is served Thursday through Sundays. The menu changes weekly; diners may call to determine the menu before reserving.

Guests come from all over the world to visit nearby Ano Nuevo State Reserve, where, from December through March, hundreds of seal elephants come to the shore for the breeding season.

*Accommodations:* 12 rooms, 9 with private bath. *Pets and children:* Not permitted. *Driving Instructions:* From San Francisco, take Route 101 south to Route 92 and turn west to Half Moon Bay. Make a left at the first light; the hotel is in the second block on the right-hand side.

## Healdsburg, California

### CAMELLIA INN

211 North Street, Healdsburg, CA 95448. 707-433-8182. *Innkeepers:* Ray and Del Lewand. Open all year.

Camellia Inn is an Italianate Victorian town house built in 1869 by Ransom Powell, one of the early settlers of Healdsburg. The house was purchased at the turn of the century by Dr. J. Walter Seawell, who made it the town's first hospital. The Seawell family occupied the town house until 1969. After a decade of other ownership it was purchased by the current innkeepers, who renamed the building in honor of the varieties of camellias flourishing in its gardens.

Typical of the Italianate period are the inn's tall ceilings and elaborate fireplaces. The double parlors have twin white-marble fireplaces. A tall hand-carved mahogany fireplace dominates one end of the dining room. In the guest rooms are fresh flowers, Oriental rugs, fluffy towels, and gift-wrapped soaps. Some have fireplaces and Jacuzzis for two. Each room pays tribute through its name to a type of camellia.

Complimentary breakfast at Camellia includes fresh fruit, soft-boiled eggs, freshly baked fruit and nut breads, juice, Viennese coffee, tea, homemade jams, and butter. The inn has a swimming pool and is two blocks from the town plaza.

*Accommodations:* 9 rooms, 7 with private bath. *Pets and smoking:* Not permitted. *Driving Instructions:* From Route 101 North, turn off on Healdsburg Avenue. North Street is the third light off Healdsburg.

## GRAPE LEAF INN

539 Johnson Street, Healdsburg, CA 95448. 707-433-8140. *Innkeeper:* Karen Sweet. Open all year.

This Victorian house, a tribute to the almighty grape, is decorated inside and out with the colors of California's wine country—lavender, purple, and gray. Each guest room bears the name and colors of one of California's great varietal grapes. Guests can sleep in Zinfandel, Cabernet, Chardonnay, or Sauvignon Blanc splendor. These rooms, as well as the spacious living room and country kitchen, are furnished with antiques chosen to re-create the feeling of the house as it must have been when it was built in 1900. Some guest rooms have stained-glass windows with overhead skylights and whirlpool baths for two.

Local wines with cheese and crackers are served in the living room by the fireplace in cool weather, or out on the veranda in summer. Breakfasts here, which include juice, fresh fruit, special egg dishes, freshly baked muffins and coffee cake, and Grape Leaf's special blend of coffee, are enjoyed in the parlor.

*Accommodations:* 7 rooms with private bath. *Pets, smoking, and children:* Not permitted. *Driving Instructions:* From the south, take Route 101 and get off at the second Healdsburg exit. Proceed 1.5 miles to Grant Street, turn right, and go two blocks to Johnson Street.

## MADRONA MANOR, A COUNTRY INN

1001 Westside Road, Healdsburg, California. Mailing address: P.O. Box 818, Healdsburg, CA 95448. 707-433-4231. *Innkeepers:* John and Carol Muir. Open all year.

Madrona Manor, a 17-room, Gothic Victorian mansion built in 1881 overlooking the valley, has an ornate entryway, a tree-lined drive, 8 acres of landscaped grounds, and a tower and many steeply pitched dormers trimmed in gingerbread. Guests enter the reception hall, with its grand staircase and adjoining parlors, dining rooms, and music room, all filled with Victorian antiques. Guest rooms in the mansion offer a night in a setting of carved beds, armoires, marble-topped bureaus, comforters, and upholstered chaises. The third floor rooms have reproductions, and more modern accommodations are found in the gingerbreaded Carriage House. A swimming pool is available.

The restaurant, which has won accolades from critics, is the domain of the innkeepers' son, Todd, a disciple of Alice Waters of the Chez Panisse and a graduate of the California Culinary Academy. It is open for dinner and Sunday brunch; a full European breakfast is served.

*Accommodations:* 20 rooms and suites with private bath. *Driving Instructions:* Take U.S. 101 north from San Francisco. Take the second Healdsburg exit. Go north to the first stop light. Turn left onto Mill Street, which becomes Westside Road. Enter through the white arches of Madrona Manor.

## THE RAFORD HOUSE

10630 Wohler Road, Healdsburg, CA 95448. 707-887-9573. *Innkeepers:* Gretchen Gustufson. Open all year.

The Raford House, now a County Historic Landmark, was built in 1880 for the owner of the largest hop ranch in the area. Its upper floor was originally the owner's quarters, and the lower floor sheltered the harvest workers. Although the original hop kilns were later removed, photographs in the inn's "history hall" show much of the past farm activity. Today, the hop fields have been replaced by the vineyards so important to the area's commerce, and the Raford House has a view of a valley of vineyards across from the front porch. Inside, the guest rooms are furnished with iron, brass, or Victorian wooden bedsteads. Two rooms have wood-burning fireplaces. Bright colors heighten the cheerful atmosphere. A combination sitting and dining room has English cottage furniture in front of its hearth. Breakfast is served here in the morning. Although this is the only meal served, there are restaurants nearby.

*Accommodations:* 7 rooms, 5 with private bath. *Pets and children:* Not permitted. *Smoking:* Restricted. *Driving Instructions:* Take U.S. 101 north from San Francisco past Santa Rosa; exit west on River Road. Drive 8 miles on River Road and turn right on Wohler Road. The inn is 1/2 mile down the road.

## Inverness, California

### TEN INVERNESS WAY

10 Inverness Way, Inverness, California. Mailing address: P.O. Box 63, Inverness, CA 94937. 415-669-1648. *Innkeeper:* Mary Davies. Open all year.

Ten Inverness Way is a large redwood-shingled house set in a lush bower of fruit trees, wisteria vines, and a hodgepodge of flower and herb gardens ringed by tall shade trees. Many garden delights find their way into the inn, in the form of fresh fruits and herbs at breakfast in the sun room, or as bowls of potpourri from the lavender and roses and fresh flowers scattered throughout. Guests and innkeeper become friends in a short time, usually at breakfast over blackberry buckwheat pancakes or Mary's cheese-scrambled eggs or, in the evening, around the fireplace and old player piano in the paneled living room. Most antiques in the inn are family pieces that enhance the "visit with friends in the country" atmosphere. Mary can help guests choose a restaurant for meals other than breakfast and will steer them to the best hikes and beaches of Point Reyes National Seashore nearby. Guests return to antique beds and handmade quilts.

*Accommodations:* 4 rooms with private bath. *Pets and smoking:* Not permitted. *Children:* Inquire first. *Driving Instructions:* From Route 1 in Olema, turn west on Bear Valley Road. At the stop sign turn left onto Sir Francis Drake Boulevard and drive to Inverness. Turn left at the Inverness Inn Restaurant and look for the Ten Inverness Way sign on the right.

*Ione, California*

## THE HEIRLOOM INN

214 Shakeley Lane, Ione, California. Mailing address: P.O. Box 322, Ione, CA 95640. 209-274-4468. *Innkeepers:* Patricia Cross & Melisande Hubbs. Open all year except Thanksgiving & Christmas.

In the peaceful foothills of the Sierra mountains nestle many hamlets and villages that sprang up during the Gold Rush. Ione, a supply center to the surrounding gold fields, was founded by some of those long-ago gold seekers. The Heirloom Inn was built in the mid-1860s as the private home of an early settler who obviously had enjoyed success in his gold dealings. The brick building features classic architectural details typical of the antebellum period. The carefully restored Heirloom Inn is hidden among tall trees and hedges on an acre.

One guest room has a working fireplace; three open onto verandas overlooking the garden. A complimentary full breakfast is served in the dining room, where a fire burns on chilly mornings. Guests may request breakfast served in bed, out on their own verandas, or in the garden. A hand-crafted adobe cottage has two additional rooms, one with early-American antiques and the other with early-California decor.

*Accommodations:* 6 rooms, 4 with private bath. *Pets and smoking:* Not permitted. *Children:* Under 10 not permitted. *Driving Instructions:* From I-5, take Route 12 to Route 88 east to Route 124. Ione is at the intersection of Routes 124 and 104. From Sacramento take Highway 16.

*Jackson, California*

## ANN MARIE'S COUNTRY INN

410 Stasal Street, Jackson, California. Mailing address: P.O. Box DN, Jackson, CA 95642. 209-223-1452. *Innkeeper:* Alberta Thomas. Open all year.

During the height of the gold-mining era, Jackson's village doctor was one James Wilson, who, in 1892, built the fishscale-shingled residence that is now Ann Marie's. Overnight guests are welcome to relax in the parlor or on the inn's front porch. Each of the inn's air-conditioned guest rooms has special touches: A collection of European dolls resides in Doll Room, for example, while a queen-size brass bed and pot-bellied stove is the focal point of a private cottage.

A full breakfast including fruit, home-baked breads, egg dishes, and home-fried potatoes is served to guests. Art works and ceramics from local artists and craftspersons are displayed throughout.

*Accommodations:* 4 rooms, 3 with private bath; 1 cottage. *Pets and smoking:* Not permitted. *Children:* Welcome. *Driving instructions:* Take Route 49, bearing left after the first stop sign in town to North Main Street, go 1 block to the first stop sign, turn right, go to the first intersection, and turn left on Stasal.

The Court = Street = Inn, Jackson Ca (est. 1870)

## THE COURT STREET INN

215 Court Street, Jackson, CA 95642. 209-223-0416. *Innkeepers:* Mardell and Bill Mart. Open all year.

The Court Street Inn's original two rooms were built in Gold Rush days by mine-owner and saloon-keeper Edward Muldoon. About thirty years later, Emily Blair, owner of the Wells Fargo and Jackson Water Works, completed the house.

The Court Street Inn is a simple home typical of most Gold Rush construction. Its front hall is dominated by a redwood stairway and paneled staircase. The parlor has a marble fireplace and is furnished with high Victorian pieces. The rest of the furnishings range in antiquity from 1700 through about 1920. One bedroom has a working fireplace with oak mantel, and another has a sunporch–sitting room with wicker furniture and plants. Breakfast is served on the porch, on the patio, or in guests' rooms. A spa is available for guests. The former backhouse, once an Indian museum, has two guest rooms sharing a bath and a large fireplace.

*Accommodations:* 8 rooms, 4 with private bath. *Children:* Under 12 not permitted. *Driving Instructions:* Jackson is at the intersection of Routes 88 and 49, southeast of Sacramento.

## GATE HOUSE INN

1330 Jackson Gate Road, Jackson, CA 95642. 209-223-3500. *Innkeepers:* Bev and Stan Smith. Open all year.

Gate House Inn is a turn-of-the-century Victorian on an acre of property surrounded by dogwoods, crepe myrtle, camellias, and walnut trees. Also tucked into the grounds is a summer house with one guest suite, a swimming pool, a greenhouse, and a screened-in barbecue room.

The mansion combines Victorian antiques with Persian rugs that cover its oak parquet floors, crystal chandeliers, and marble fireplaces. The Bridal Suite has a working tiled fireplace and looks out on the gardens. Wood Room, once the cook's quarters when Gate House was a private residence, is done in old woods.

Breakfast is served in nice weather on the screened-in porch. Gate House is surrounded by pasture land but is with an easy walk of several fine restaurants.

*Accommodations:* 5 rooms with private bath. *Pets and smoking:* Not permitted. *Driving Instructions:* Take Route 49 to Jackson, where Main Street becomes Jackson Gate Road; the inn is 2 miles north of Jackson.

*Jamestown, California*

## JAMESTOWN HOTEL

18153 Main Street, Jamestown, California. Mailing address: P.O. Box 539, Jamestown, CA 95327. 209-984-3902. *Innkeepers:* Michael and Marcia Walsh. Open all year except Christmas.

The Jamestown Hotel is a typical Western brick hotel with full-front wooden balcony and front porch. Its guest rooms are named after famous Western luminaries of the period and are decorated with antique furnishings. Each boasts a Victorian bathroom with an old claw-footed tub and a marble-topped sink. The Lotta Crabtree suite features a fancy iron bedstead, Laura Ashley prints, and a separate sitting room with wicker furniture. One suite has a painted iron bed, black claw-footed bathtub, and period sitting room.

The Jamestown Hotel has gained a reputation for its luncheons, Sunday champagne brunch, and dinners, available to the general public as well as guests and served, optionally, on the enclosed patio from April through October.

*Accommodations:* 8 rooms with private bath. *Pets:* Not permitted. *Children:* Under 8 not permitted. *Driving Instructions:* Take Route 108 about 50 miles east from Modesto to Jamestown.

## THE PALM HOTEL

10382 Willow Street, Jamestown, CA 95327. 209-984-3429. *Innkeeper:* Jacob Barendregt. Open all year.

The Palm, named for the tall palm tree standing guard at the entrance, is a fanciful, gabled Victorian-style building complete with a four-story tower and two small porches. It was built in the 1890s as a private home and later enlarged to serve as a boarding house for miners and railroad men.

The Palm has been restored and decorated by Jacob Barendregt and his family, its rooms furnished with Victorian antiques of wicker, oak, and walnut. The lobby has a marble-top bar that doubles as a reception desk and a buffet table where a full breakfast is served. Some guest rooms have sitting areas tucked into the tower bay windows, while most have beds that are covered with soft comforters and have eyelet dust ruffles. Those who use the shared bathroom will not be disappointed with the plethora of soft towels and extensive use of marble, including the double shower.

*Accommodations:* 9 rooms, 5 with private bath. *Pets:* Not permitted. *Smoking:* Restricted to certain areas. *Driving instructions:* Take Route 108 or Route 120 to Jamestown. The inn is one block off Main Street.

## STILLWATER COVE RANCH

22555 Highway 1, Jenner, CA 95450. 707-847-3227. *Innkeeper:* Linda Rudy. Open all year except at Christmas.

Linda Rudy has converted the old Stillwater Cove Ranch into a collection of accommodations perched above the rocky cliffs of this coastal village. The ranch was first formed in 1931 as a private school for boys under the direction of Mr. and Mrs. Paul P. Rudy. For about thirty-five years, some fifty boys were boarded there and educated in ranch life and academic subjects. In 1966, Mrs. Rudy closed the school and began its conversion into a guest ranch.

The school consisted of a number of separate units designed to meet a particular school need, and the inn currently reflects these origins. There are separate cottages known as Teacher's Cottage and Cook's Cottage, as well as an East Room, West Room, Science Room, King Room, and Dairy Barn. The last is a large bunkhouse of interest to touring groups. All the units but the King Room have fireplaces, and wood is included in the price. Rooms are large, airy, and quite attractive. Cook's Cottage, for example, has exposed beams, a stone fireplace, wall-to-wall carpeting, and white wicker furniture.

At present, the inn does not offer meals to transient guests. It does, however, make its extensive kitchen facilities available to the many large groups (twenty-five to forty persons) that frequently book the facilities, including wedding parties. Linda is a noted cook who, on special occasions, will do group family-style meals. On some three-day weekends cooking classes are offered at the ranch. Several times Julia Child has been guest chef. Photography workshops are also available, as are seminars and retreats. For information about the classes and for reservations for them, call the inn.

*Accommodations:* 6 guest rooms with private bath, plus a bunkhouse with 8 bunks. *Driving Instructions:* The inn is 16 miles north of Jenner on Route 1.

## JULIAN GOLD RUSH HOTEL

2032 Main Street, Julian, California. Mailing address: P.O. Box 1856, Julian, CA 92036. 619-765-0201. *Innkeepers:* Steve and Gig Ballinger. Open all year.

Gold was discovered here in 1870, and by 1880 it was a full-blown gold-dust town, a sea of tents and shacks with, in its heyday, a total of fifteen hotels. One of them was the Hotel Robinson, later to be renamed the Julian Gold Rush Hotel.

The hotel's original name dates to its initial construction by a freed Georgia slave, Albert Robinson, who had come to the area with his former master, Major Chase. In time, Robinson established himself as a cook and met and married Margaret Tull, also a cook. With a modest capital advance from the major and their pooled savings, they opened a small but popular restaurant where Southern cooking and apple pie were specialties of the house. Later the popularity of the restaurant prompted the Robinsons to expand their operation into a small hotel. They even managed to import two bathtubs, shipped all the way around the Horn.

Today, the hotel is listed in the National Register of Historic Places and is maintained as it was at its Victorian peak. Rooms are furnished with such antiques as brass beds, 6-foot-high oak beds, and homespun comforters. The walls have attractive Victorian wallpaper and old-fashioned wood moldings. Most guest rooms still share the "necessary" rooms at the ends of the halls. The lobby has a wood-burning stove and comfortable chairs conveying an atmosphere of hospitality and warmth.The Ballingers have restored the dining room, where breakfast, the only meal, is served to houseguests.

In addition to the rooms in the main hotel, there are a separate patio cottage and the Honeymoon House, built in the 1940s, with one bedroom, a wood-burning fireplace, wicker furniture, and lace curtains. Breakfast is served only to houseguests.

*Accommodations:* 18 rooms; 4 with private bath, 13 sharing 4 baths; 2 cottages. *Pets:* Not permitted. *Children:* Permitted on weekdays only. *Driving Instructions:* The town of Julian can be reached by Route 78-79.

## CARRIAGE HOUSE

1322 Catalina Street, Laguna Beach, CA 92651. 714-494-8945. *Innkeepers:* Dee and Vernon Taylor. Open all year.

This guest house was built in the 1920s in the style of a colonial carriage house. The two-story building surrounding a brick courtyard filled with lush green plants and a large tiered fountain is in many ways reminiscent of both New Orleans and New England. Carriage House was owned for a time by movie mogul Louis B. Mayer, and it is thought that he was responsible for placing the New England-style cupola on the roof of the building. The inn is just a few houses away from the ocean.

Over the decades, Laguna Beach has been a popular retreat for those living in Los Angeles and San Diego. Carriage House once contained several local art galleries, and a portion of the first floor was used by a woman who baked pies for a local bakery. Her kitchen is now the inn's "Lilac Time" suite. Pleated fabrics provide a backdrop and a canopy to a polished-brass bed in this room. French doors lead to the courtyard, and the bathroom retains its original claw-footed tub. Several of the five other suites have two bedrooms, a sitting room, and a complete kitchen. A complimentary bottle of wine and a basket of fresh fruit await guests upon arrival, and sherry is provided for an evening nightcap. Breakfast is served in the dining room or out under the carrotwood tree in the courtyard.

*Accommodations:* 6 suites with private bath. *Pets:* Not permitted. *Driving Instructions:* Take the Laguna Freeway (Route 133) west to the Coast Highway. Drive South to Cress Street, turn left, and go two blocks to Catalina Street.

## CASA LAGUNA INN

2510 South Coast Highway, Laguna Beach, CA 92651. 714-494-2996. *Innkeeper:* Jerry and Luanne Siegel. Open all year. Casa Laguna Inn is a terraced complex of tropical gardens, palm trees, and California Mission and Spanish Revival buildings. The heart of this sprawling inn is the Mission House and the Cottage, built in the 1930s to provide guest accommodations for Frank Miller's historic Villa Rockledge. In the 1940s nineteen casitas were added, each with views of the garden courtyard, the swimming pool, or the Pacific beyond. In the evening, sunsets and the lights of Avalon on distant Santa Catalina Island can be seen.

The inn is decorated in a comfortably eclectic manner, with antiques and contemporary furnishings equally at home amid antique tile-work and lush plantings. The Library is a favorite gathering spot, where breakfast, afternoon tea, wine, and hors d'oeuvres are served. Guests are welcome to enjoy the aviary and ocean views from the bell tower. Two beaches are across from the inn—one white and sandy, the other, with coves and tidal pools. Deep sea fishing, golf, and tennis are easily arranged. The inns regularly hosts art exhibits and wine tastings.

*Accommodations:* 20 rooms and suites with private bath. *Pets:* Not permitted. *Driving instructions:* The inn is on the Pacific Coast Highway in Laguna Beach, south of Newport Beach.

*La Jolla, California*

## BED AND BREAKFAST INN AT LA JOLLA

7753 Draper Avenue, La Jolla, CA 92037. 619-456-2066. *Innkeeper:* Ardath Albee. Open all year.

The Bed and Breakfast inn is in the heart of La Jolla's cultural complex, across from the Museum of Contemporary Art. Designed by architect Irving Gill for a wealthy industrialist, the 1913 house was later the home of the John Phillip Sousa family for seven years. When the current owner tackled the extensive renovation in 1984, six guest rooms were added. Each is furnished in cottage decor, with antiques used throughout. A subdued color scheme of whites and beiges sets off the richness of the Oriental carpets. Flowers, fruit baskets, and sherry await guests in their rooms. Three guest rooms have views of the ocean, a block away; three rooms have working fireplaces. Wine and cheese are served in late afternoon.

*Accommodations:* 16 rooms, 15 with private bath. *Pets and smoking:* Not permitted. *Children:* Under 12 not permitted. *Driving Instructions:* From San Diego, take Route 5 north to the Ardath Road exit; continue to Torrey Pines Road. Bear left and proceed to Prospect Place. Turn right and go 10 blocks to Draper Avenue. Turn left.

## Little River, California

# GLENDEVEN

8221 North Highway 1, Little River, CA 95456. 707-937-0083. *Innkeepers:* Jan and Janet deVries. Open all year.

Glendeven is a small country guest house just south of Mendocino, overlooking the dramatic north coast of California. Built in 1867 by Isaiah Stevens of Maine, the building reflects the strong New England character which attracted settlers to this area following the discovery of the redwood forests. In 1977 the home was purchased by designers Jan and Janet deVries, who created Glendeven on this headland meadow.

The deVries have blended antique furnishings with their collection of more contemporary paintings, prints, and ceramics. Many rooms have working fireplaces, and most have private baths. The Garret is tucked up under the eaves on the third floor, with dormers that offer views of the bay. Eastlin, on the first floor, has a sitting room with French doors that open onto the porch and its own fireplace. Other rooms are in Stevencroft.

The day at Glendeven begins with a breakfast of fresh fruit, home--baked breads, eggs, and coffee or tea, all of which may be served in either the main sitting room, with its brick fireplace, or in one's room.

*Accommodations:* 10 rooms, 8 with private bath; 1 suite. *Pets and smoking:* Not permitted. *Children:* Under 8 not permitted. *Driving instructions:* The guest house is on Route 1, about 1 1/2 miles south of Mendocino.

## HERITAGE HOUSE

Highway 1, Little River, CA 95456. 707-937-5885. *Innkeeper:* Gay Dennen Moore. Open February through November.

On a rugged stretch of the Mendocino coastline, Heritage House is a collection of buildings dating back to 1877. The original farmhouse was constructed for the Pullen family by John Dennen, ancestor of the current innkeeper. Over the years, the property has served as a base for smuggling — liquor during Prohibition, and goods and people from the Orient — and as a hideout for the renowned bandit Baby Face Nelson. A secret cave used by smugglers is nearby.

Accommodations are mostly in a group of cottages tucked unobtrusively into the landscape. Many of the furnishings date from the mid-nineteenth century and have been collected over the years since the Dennens purchased the property. Some were made in the Mendocino area by local craftsmen, and others were imported by early settlers who brought them by ship around the Horn. One building, the Apple House Lounge, is an old apple-storage barn that was dismantled on its site 24 miles away in Glen Blair and reassembled adjacent to the main farmhouse. The large stone fireplace, wide-board wall paneling, and sturdy beams add to the flavor of this popular gathering spot at Heritage House. One may choose from suites in the old water tower or cottages at the edge of the sea cliffs.

Meals are served in a long dining room bordered with a wall of windows overlooking the coastline. The menu changes daily and offers a choice of three entrées.

*Accommodations:* 69 rooms with private bath, ranging from singles to sitting-room suites. *Pets:* Not permitted. *Driving Instructions:* The inn is 15 miles south of Fort Bragg on Route 1.

## THE VICTORIAN FARMHOUSE

7001 North Highway 1, Little River, California. Mailing address: P.O. Box 357, Little River, CA 95456. 707-937-0697. *Innkeepers:* Carole and George Molnar. Open all year.

The Victorian Farmhouse, built in 1877 by John and Emma Dora Dennen, is on the Pacific coast surrounded by several acres of flowers, trees, fields, and an apple orchard. George's hobby is antique clocks, and Carole's is Victorian toys, which are displayed throughout the inn. The parlor is a favorite get-together spot where sherry is served in the evening.

Upstairs a Victorian sitting room has views of the redwoods and the flower garden behind the inn. Off it are the Emma Dora Room and the Dennen Room, both guest rooms with ocean views and unusual redwood ceilings. The Garden Room downstairs has a private entrance and its own flower garden, as well as a luxurious redwood bathroom. All beds are covered by antique quilts. Breakfast, including muffins or breads and fresh fruit, is brought to each room. The inn is two doors from a fine restaurant and is with an easy stroll is a secluded cove on the rugged, wave-battered coast.

*Accommodations:* 10 rooms, 6 with private bath and fireplaces. *Pets and smoking:* Not permitted. *Children:* Under 11 not permitted. *Driving Instructions:* 3 miles south of Mendocino on Route 1.

## Los Angeles, California

## SALISBURY HOUSE

2273 West Twentieth Street, Los Angeles, CA 90018. 213-737-7817.
*Innkeepers:* Sue and Jay German. Open all year.

Salisbury House is a classic 1909 California Craftsman–style home in quiet residential neighborhood. Each guest room has antique beds and dressers with special homey touches. One room features a sunny window seat with antique dolls sitting on the seat cushion. The American suite occupies the entire third floor, with eaves, gables, and a sitting area.

There is a working fireplace in the beamed living room, and a full breakfast, served in the formal dining room, includes fresh fruit, juice, home-baked goods and an entreé.

*Accommodations:* 5 rooms, 3 with private bath. *Pets and smoking:* Not permitted. *Children:* Under 11 not permitted. *Driving Instructions:* From the Santa Monica Freeway (I-10) go north one block on Western Avenue, then turn left on Twentieth Street.

## TERRACE MANOR

1353 Alvarado Terrace, Los Angeles, CA 90006. 213-381-1478. *Innkeepers:* Sandy and Shirley Spillman. Open all year.

The large, three story, Tudor-style Terrace Manor stands as a reminder of the past. It was built in 1903 for Robert Raphael, owner of a glass factory, and retains many of its original, elaborate leaded and Art Nouveau stained-glass windows and its unusual wall panels of mahogany and rare tiger oak. Against such backdrops the Spillmans have placed their collections of period antiques and Victorian memorabilia. Old Caruso recordings add to the atmosphere, and stereoscopic pictures are set out in the library. Many collectibles grace the guest rooms, each decorated around a theme, incorporating romantic wallpapers, antiques, and coordinated linens and dust ruffles. One room, Collector's Corner, features Shirley's figurine perfume bottle collection. A special egg dish or pancakes are served for breakfast in the dining room, which has an Ionic-columned fireplace. Sandy, a member of a unique private club, the Hollywood Magic Castle, performs magic tricks for guests. Reservations can be made for guests to visit the Magic Castle.

*Accommodations:* 5 rooms with private bath. *Pets and smoking:* Not permitted. *Children:* Under 10 not permitted. *Driving Instructions:* From the San Diego Freeway (405), exit to the Santa Monica Freeway (10) going east. Take the Hoover off-ramp and turn left on Hoover. Drive a mile to Alvarado Terrace and turn right.

## TAMARACK LODGE RESORT

Twin Lakes Road, Mammoth Lakes, California. Mailing address: Box 69, Mammoth Lakes, CA 93546. 619-934-2442. *Innkeepers:* David and Carol Watson. Open all year. Restaurant closes for two brief periods; call first.

The Tamarack Lodge Resort is in the midst of John Muir country at an altitude of 8,600 feet, just south of Yosemite National Park and about 12 miles from the Devils Postpile National Monument, surrounded by what the famous naturalist called the "most beautiful mountain range in the world." The lodge was constructed in 1924 and has accepted guests ever since.

The restaurant, with a spectacular view of the lakes and waterfalls, is open to the public for all three meals. There is a large rock fireplace in the lobby, a popular gathering spot.

Guests staying in the cabins can buy provisions at the general store in Twin Lakes in the summer and in Mammoth Village all year. In the winter months there is a complete cross-country skiing center at the lodge. Mammoth Ski Area is a major downhill center, with two gondolas, twenty-six chair lifts, and many miles of runs. In the summer, guests can explore at least ten lakes with a 5-mile radius. At the lodge itself are boating and fishing in Twin Lakes.

*Accommodations:* 12 rooms, 5 with private bath, and 22 housekeeping cabins. *Pets:* Not permitted. *Smoking:* Cabins only. *Driving Instructions:* Take Route 395 to Highway 203 north of Bishop. Go about 2 1/2 miles through Mammoth Lakes. Route 203 becomes Lake Mary Road. Take the right fork on Twin Lakes Road,

*Mendocino, California*

## THE HEADLANDS INN

Albion and Howard Streets, Mendocino, California. Mailing address: P.O. Box 132, Mendocino, CA 95460. 707-937-4431. *Innkeepers:* Pat and Rod Stofle. Open all year.

The Headlands Inn began as a small barber shop. In 1873 the barber added a second story to house his growing family, and in succeeding years the building served as a saloon and as an annex to the old Wilson Hotel. The Headlands Inn now has been lovingly restored to a charm that outdoes any of its previous guises. Pat and Rod maintain a relaxed, informal atmosphere. The inn actually looks like a New England transplant, thanks to the influence of the New England loggers who settled in the Mendocino area in the mid-nineteenth century.

Each guest room has its own special characteristics, including antiques, a king- or queen-size bed, and a sitting area, with a wood-burning fireplace. Three have a sofa; two have overstuffed chairs and ocean views. Third-floor rooms boast window seats in the dormers, on which to sit and look out over the Pacific coastline and the seaside village. The cottage nearby has been restored and has a four-poster bed, a fireplace, and old-fashioned overstuffed chairs. There are two Victorian parlors.

Breakfast includes Pat's blueberry muffins and one of fourteen different hot entrées that varies each day, fruits, and beverages. An English-style garden provides flowers for the rooms.

*Accommodations:* 5 rooms with private bath. *Pets, smoking, and children:* Not permitted. *Driving Instructions:* Mendocino is can be reached from Route 1. The inn is 2 blocks from the center of the village.

## JOSHUA GRINDLE INN

44800 Little Lake Road, Mendocino, California. Mailing address: P.O. Box 647, Mendocino, CA 95460. 707-937-4143. *Innkeepers:* Jim and Arlene Moorehead. Open all year.

Like most of his fellow townsmen, Joshua Grindle was a transplanted New Englander. He arrived from Maine in 1869 to make his fortune in the fast-emerging redwood lumber business. And, like his fellow workers, most of his energy was, at first, devoted to the effort of establishing his business rather than looking after his personal needs. It was not until 1879 that he chose a wife, Alice Hills, and began construction of their house on a plot of land given to them by his bride's family. Sadly, Alice was not to see the house completed; she died in childbirth in early 1882. Her son survived, and Grindle continued to live in the house until his death in 1928. The house did not leave the hands of the Grindle descendants until 1967.

On two acres in the village, the inn comprises guest accommodations, a parlor, and a dining room, in a building clearly reflecting Joshua Grindle's New England heritage. It is filled with a collection of early American antiques from the eighteenth and nineteenth centuries. There are many etchings, oil paintings, and serigraphs. Six guest rooms have working fireplaces.

Guest rooms come in all sizes and shapes. Two rooms, each with

a fireplace and early pine furnishings, are in a saltbox cottage, and a 30-foot-high "Mendocino-style" water tower has three rooms, two with fireplaces.

Breakfast is served in the dining room on a 10-foot 6-inch pine harvest table that dates from about 1830. The meal itself is "English style," with homemade sconces or muffins, boiled egg, fresh fruit, juice, and coffee or tea. In the early evening many guests like to gather in the parlor to enjoy the fire, play the baby grand piano, read, have a game of backgammon or chess, or talk of the day's exploring. The inn provides cream sherry and fruit on the hunt board.

*Accommodations:* 10 rooms with private bath. *Pets and smoking:* Not permitted. *Children:* Under 11 not permitted. *Driving Instructions:* Turn west on Route 128, just north of Cloverdale. This takes you out to the coast and Route 1. Go 12 miles north to Mendocino. The inn is on the corner of Route 1 and Little Lake Road.

## THE MAC CALLUM HOUSE INN

45020 Albion Street, Mendocino, California. Mailing address: P.O. Box 206, Mendocino, CA 95460. 707-937-0289 *Innkeepers:* Melanie and Joe Reding. Open all year.

As you walk up the brick path and broad steps bounded by tubs of flowering plants to the Mac Callum House Inn, a sounding whale, carved from a single log, guards the walk on your left. The front of the Victorian mansion is dominated by an elaborate single eave centered over the door, which in turn is flanked by a multipaned sun parlor and a New England-style porch. The house was built as a wedding present for Daisy Mac Callum, who lived there for more than forty-five years until her death in the early 1950s. Part of the warmth that emanates from the house comes from Daisy's furnishings.

In 1974 the comfortable country home was transformed into an equally comfortable inn, complete with main house and newly out-fitted carriage house, barn, old greenhouse, garden gazebo, and water tower, all of which have overnight accommodations. Each guest room has its distinct flavor: one is covered from stem to stern with redwood paneling and wainscoting; another has old-fashioned floral striped wallpaper; in still another, white wicker sets the theme. One room has a king-size canopied bed and a private bath.

A happy way to relax in the late afternoon is to sit in the filtered light of the sun parlor enjoying a cup of tea or a glass of wine. After 6 P.M., one may move to the dining room to enjoy a dinner in which only the freshest foods are served. The dinner menu lists about ten items. Typical fare is rack of lamb, medallions of beef Bordelaise, roast game hen, lemon veal, veal champignons, or poached salmon with bearnaise sauce. Specials of the day augment the basic list and include fresh fish and a vegetarian entrée. For starters guests may choose between homemade French onion soup, Mac Callum House mushrooms, escargots, and oysters casino.

*Accommodations:* 20 rooms, 7 with private bath, the others sharing baths. *Pets:* Not permitted. *Driving Instructions:* The Mac Callum House is in the center of the village.

## MENDOCINO HOTEL

45080 Main Street, Mendocino, California. Mailing address: P.O. Box 587, Mendocino, CA 95460. 707-937-0511. *Innkeeper:* Paul Cadelago. Open all year.

In 1878 Ben Bever decided to turn his Main Street home into a hotel. He had the house moved back from the street to accommodate a large new addition, had a schoonerful of furnishings shipped around Cape Horn from the East, and opened the Temperance House, assuring that "no liquor will be served." Through the years the hotel underwent changes—new owners, new names, additions, wings, and an old-West false front. After a full year of restoration, the historic old hotel opened its doors in 1975 as one of the most elegant museum-like hotels on the coast. Ben Bever and his early successors surely wouldn't recognize the place. The hotel has elaborate stained-glass and leaded windows, polished hardwood floors covered by Oriental rugs, and posh Victorian furnishings. A sculptured eighteenth-century steel fireplace and a Tiffany stained-glass dome are the outstanding additions. The dome is suspended over a carved bar—no more temperance here! The public rooms are wallpapered with red flocked papers and furnished with period antiques. The guest rooms have floral wallpaper, canopied or brass beds, and marble-topped bureaus. Some of the rooms open onto the

balcony overlooking the ocean just a few yards down the street. The hotel's restaurant serves breakfast, lunch, and dinner on its glassed-in garden patio, as well as in its Victorian dining room. Room service is available.

There are now twenty-five additional rooms housed in four garden cottages behind the hotel. One cottage was built in 1852 by an early Mendocino settler. Many rooms have fireplaces, marble baths, and television sets.

*Accommodations:* 26 rooms, 13 with private bath; 25 rooms in 4 garden cottages. *Pets:* Not permitted. *Driving Instructions:* Take U.S. 101 north to Route 128, drive west on 128 to Route 1, and take Route 1 north about 6 miles to Mendocino.

## MENDOCINO VILLAGE INN

Main Street, Mendocino, California. Mailing address: Box 626, Mendocino, CA 95460. 707-937-0246. *Innkeepers:* Sue and Tom Allen. Open all year.

The Mendocino Village Inn, completely restored in 1986, is an 1882 Queen–Anne Victorian home that was built as the private residence of the town doctor. The decor is an eclectic blend of Victorian and country furnishings and the Allens' collection of contemporary art. Seven guest rooms have working fireplaces. Full breakfasts of fruits and freshly baked breads are served with a main dish such as herbed cheesecake or blue cornmeal banana pancakes. Across the street is a path that leads down to the beach and along the bluffs, which overlook the sea. This is a great spot for watching migrating whales or picking wild berries. Restaurants and shops are with walking distance.

*Accommodations:* 12 rooms, 10 with private bath. *Pets and smoking:* Not permitted. *Children:* Under 10 discouraged. *Driving Instructions:* Mendocino is 3 hours north of San Francisco on Route 1.

## WHITEGATE INN

499 Howard, Mendocino, California. Mailing address: P.O. Box 150, Mendocino, CA 95460. 707-937-4892. *Innkeeper:* Patricia and John Valletta. Open all year.

Overlooking the Mendocino Headlands State Park, where hiking trails lead along the cliffs to secluded beaches below, is the Whitegate Inn, an 1880 Victorian home. One of Mendocino's more elegant structures, it sits behind a tidy row of picket fencing and flower gardens.

Whitegate is decorated throughout with Victorian antiques. The parlor, more formal than we prefer for comfortable lounging, has an original crystal chandelier that illuminates the ornate gilded moldings.

In the afternoon, guests are invited to the parlor to share a glass of wine and watch the sunset. Guest rooms have Victorian floral wallpapers and antique beds that have down comforters and lacy sheets. Each has its own sitting area; several have ocean views and a fireplace. Pat serves a full breakfast in the formal dining room; it may be the best we have had at any inn, beautifully presented, with eggs florentine, warm bran muffins and and herb bread, jam and marmalade, coffee, and a variety of herb and regular teas. French doors in the dining room open to a deck and gazebo.

*Accommodations:* 5 rooms with private bath. *Pets and smoking:* Not permitted. *Children:* Not permitted. *Driving Instructions:* In Mendocino, take Main Street to Howard Street.

## MOUNTAIN HOME INN

810 Panoramic Highway, Mill Valley, CA 94941. 415-381-9000. *Innkeeper:* Robert Green. Open all year.

Just north of San Francisco is Mt. Tamalpais, a tourist mecca for more than a century. Thousands of visitors have traveled here, at first by ferry and cow path, later via "the world's crookedest railroad," and finally by car on the scenic highway that winds past the Mountain Home Inn, the last of the magnificent hotels to serve the throngs of vacationers. Mt. Tamalpais has thousands of acres of parkland criss-crossed by trails for hikers and horseback riders, including one that leads from the inn down the mountain into the heart of Muir Woods National Monument, the majestic redwood preserve along the coast.

Mountain Home Inn, built in 1912, has been restored and expanded in a five-year, $1.5 million dollar project under the direction of architect John Deamer, a student of Paolo Soleri. Fashioned much like a miniature National Park hotel, this ten-room inn, famous for its striking views, offers elegantly rustic guest rooms, most with terraces and some with fireplaces and skylights. The restaurant (closed Monday) serves French cuisine to both guests and the public for lunch and dinner. A Continental breakfast is avaialable to guests only.

*Accommodations:* 10 rooms with private bath. *Pets:* Not permitted. *Smoking:* In lobby only. *Driving instructions:* From San Francisco, take Route 1 north to the Mill Valley exit. Drive 3 miles and turn right on Panoramic. Drive 2 1/4 miles to the inn on the east side of the road.

Rising beyond the village of Montecito are the rugged foothills of the Santa Ynez Mountains and the beautiful San Rafael Wilderness Area. There are many hiking areas and horseback riding opportunities here, and nearby Santa Barbara offers a great many recreational and sightseeing activities to tourists in the area.

## SAN YSIDRO RANCH

900 San Ysidro Lane, Montecito, CA 93108. 805-969-5046. *Innkeeper:* Michael Ullman. Open all year.

San Ysidro Ranch, a hideaway in the foothills of the Santa Ynez Mountains and one of the oldest guest resorts in California, opened to visitors in 1893. The land was originally part of a Spanish land grant, and Mission Santa Barbara padres worked the ranch early in the nineteenth century. The adobe built by the padres in 1825 still stands.

On arrival, guests find their names already engraved on a wooden plaque outside the door of their cottage accommodation. Each cottage and cottage room is in a glen hidden in foliage and flowers. Cottages vary in shape and design; some are single-unit, others contain several guest accommodations under a single roof. Most of the cottages have porches with views of the mountains or ocean. All have fireplaces, and some have kitchenettes. The deluxe Forest Cottage has a large living room with fireplace, kitchen, bedroom, private bath, deck, and private Jacuzzi.

San Ysidro began its star-studded life under Ronald Colman's ownership. The ranch was always (and still is) filled with "glitterati," seeking the peace and solitude offered here. Winston Churchill, Somerset Maugham, Sinclair Lewis, and Aldous Huxley were among those who came to write.

The Hacienda Room, in the main lounge, has game tables, comfortable couches and chairs, a big stone fireplace, and honor bar. Next door is the restaurant, formerly a citrus-packing house. The dining rooms are separated by thick stone walls with archways hewn into them. Fresh flowers, antiques, and soft candlelight create an atmosphere of elegance. The menu features light French cuisine; samplings include warm crayfish salad with oyster mushrooms and spinach; grilled sea bass with basil; and air-dried Peking duck.

San Ysidro offers plentiful recreational opportunities. There are a heated pool, tennis courts with distracting vistas of rugged mountains

and the blue Pacific, a stable full of fine quarter horses, and more than 500 acres of trail-crossed wilderness.

*Accommodations:* 43 cottage rooms and suites with private bath. *Pets:* "Well-behaved" pets are welcom (EP); horses are $30 a night (AP) and are served "gourmet hay." *Driving Instructions:* Take Route 101 for 5 miles south of Santa Barbara to the San Ysidro Road exit. Head toward the mountains on San Ysidro Road for 2 miles. Take the fork to the right at San Ysidro Lane, which ends at the ranch.

## Monterey, California

### THE JABBERWOCK

598 Laine Street, Monterey, CA 93940. 408-372-4777. *Innkeepers:* Jim and Barbara Allen. Open all year.

'All mimsy were the borogoves, and the mome raths outgrabe. . . .'' Lewis Carroll's Alice used her looking glass to figure out these mysterious words. Monterey's Jabberwock and her guest rooms, The Brillig, Mome Rath, and others have derived their names from the whimsical poem in *Through the Looking-Glass.*

Jabberwock is very near John Steinbeck's Cannery Row and the Monterey Aquarium. The house, a large 1911 Victorian complete with turrets and eaves, is surrounded by two tropical gardens fed by waterfalls. The antique-filled rooms inside make a visit memorable. All beds are piled high with pillows and goose-down comforters spread over lace-trimmed linens. Breakfasts feature Barbara's specialties. Guests gather in the parlor at 5 o'clock for sherry and hors d'oeuvres, and find milk and homemade cookies awaiting them at bedtime.

*Accommodations:* 7 rooms, 3 with private bath. *Pets, smoking, and children:* Not permitted. *Driving Instructions:* Take Route 1 to the Del Monte–Pacific Grove exit. Go through a tunnel south of Fisherman's Wharf. Turn left onto Hoffman Street, and go 2 blocks to Laine Street.

*Monterey, California*

## OLD MONTEREY INN

500 Martin Street, Monterey, CA 93490. 405-375-8284. *Innkeepers:* Ann and Gene Swett. Open all year.

The Old Monterey Inn is a Tudor-style Craftsman house built in 1920 by Carmel Martin, a former mayor of Monterey. The inn is set with English-style gardens, protected by hedges, pines, redwoods, and oaks. Stone paths lead to secluded patios and niches where guests may listen to the barking of sea lions and the sounds of the ocean in the distance.

Guests get acquainted in the living room, with its groupings of chairs and couches by the fireside, over wine and cheese in the late afternoon. Antique furnishings are the rule in guest rooms, as are oversized beds and fluffy goose-down comforters. Many guest rooms and suites have working fireplaces, stained-glass windows, and skylights. A full breakfast — Belgian waffles, quiches, cheese popovers, and other specialties — is served in guests' rooms or in the dining room, which has a copper fireplace hood and hand-painted ceiling panels.

*Accommodations:* 10 rooms with private bath. *Pets smoking, and children:* Not permitted. *Driving Instructions:* From the south, take the Munras Avenue exit from Route 1, make an immediate left at Soledad Drive, then right at Pacific Street. Go 1/2 mile to Martin Street, on the left.

## Murphys, California

### DUNBAR HOUSE, 1880

271 Jones Street, Murphys, California. Mailing address: Box 1375, Murphys, CA 95247. 209-728-2897. *Innkeepers:* Barbara and Bob Costa.

Dunbar House is in the heart of California's southern Mother Lode region, in a town that remains among the least changed since the mining days. This bed-and-breakfast inn, built in 1880, is a example of Italianate style and has been used as a vintage set on television shows. A porch around three sides of the building offers views of the tree-shaded Main Street.

Barbara and Bob Costa restored the inn, filling the rooms with their collection of antiques. Guest rooms have crocheted coverlets and comforters on the queen-size beds and woodburning stoves. The innkeepers welcome guests with a complimentary beverage — lemonade in summer, hot apple cider in winter. A full breakfast is served in the garden, in the dining room by fireside, or in guest's rooms.

*Accommodations:* 5 rooms with private bath. *Pets and smoking:* Not permitted. *Children:* Under 10 not permitted. *Driving Instructions:* Take Route 49 north of Sonora to Angels Camp (Route 4) heading northeast. Turn left at Murphys' business district. Drive to Main Street and turn left at the historical monument, behind which is the inn.

## MURPHYS HOTEL

457 Main Street, Murphys, California. Mailing address: P.O. Box 329, Murphys, CA 95247. 209-728-3444. *Innkeeper:* Robert Walker. Open all year.

Murphys Hotel is a classic old Western mining hotel complete with a "Wild West" saloon. The "Queen of the Sierra," as the hotel was first called, was built in 1855–56 by James Sperry and John Perry to accommodate visitors from all over the world who came to see the newest local tourist attraction: the Calaveras Grove of Big Trees.

Only nine of the twenty-nine guest rooms are in the hotel itself; the rest are in an adjoining motel, which has been refurbished. The rooms in the hotel are much the same as they were in Sperry and Perry's innkeeping days: The baths are still down the halls, and there is nary a phone or television to be found. President Ulysses S. Grant wouldn't notice anything unusual in his Presidential Suite today—it seems just the way he left it.

The dining room serves three meals a day to lodgers, tourists, and townspeople. Drinks are served, as they used to be, in the saloon.

*Accommodations:* 29 rooms, 20 with private bath (old hotel rooms share baths). *Pets:* Permitted. *Driving Instructions:* North of Sonora, turn off Route 49 at Angels Camp onto Route 4 heading east into the national forest. The hotel is on Main Street (off Route 4).

## BEAZLEY HOUSE

1910 First Street, Napa, CA 94559. 707-257-1649. *Innkeepers:* The
Beazley family. Open all year.

Napa has just undergone a multimillion-dollar urban-renewal face-lift
emphasizing preservation and restoration rather than destruction. The
downtown area now has a quaint "Norman Rockwell" look, with many
restored buildings but also practical additions such as convenient parking areas. New legislation permits bed-and-breakfast inns in the historic district, further encouraging the preservation of historic buildings.

A perfect example of this principle in action is the Beazley House.
Built in 1902 as the Colonial Revival shingle-style residence of a prominent surgeon, Beazley House now welcomes guests year round. The
shingled building, with its awninged windows and attractive grounds,
is noted for its woodwork and stained glass. Entering through the
stained-glass doors, guests see the building's inlaid oaken floors and

mahogany door and picture moldings. A music room is just ahead, and to the left is a spacious living room, with its large fireplace and modest library that flanks a cushioned window seat. Here, sherry and tea or coffee are served to guests from the teacart. To the right as you enter is the mahogany-paneled dining room, which, like most other rooms in the house, has a coved ceiling. Here, a full breakfast is served to guests.

A window seat and stained-glass window are nestled into a staircase that leads to six comfortable guest rooms above. The half-round window is one of the most distinctive elements of the house. Its stained-and leaded-glass throws rainbow hues onto the stairs below. Each guest room has a special feature that makes it particularly nice. The Sherry Room contains an antique cherry-wood bedroom set. The Master Bedroom has a brass bed, as well as a fireplace complete with old-fashioned gas logs. The Carriage House is a recent addition modeled after the original. Its five guest rooms have fireplaces, country quilts, and antiques. These larger rooms feature two-person spas. Beazley House is a perfect base for exploring Napa and the surrounding wine country.

*Accommodations:* 9 rooms with private bath. *Pets, smoking, and children:* Not permitted. *Driving Instructions:* On Route 29 into Napa take the Calistoga fork to the Central Napa–First Street exit. Make a left on Second Street, go 3/10 mile, and make a left on Warren and a left onto First Street. The inn is at the corner of First and Warren.

## CHURCHILL MANOR

485 Brown Street, Napa, CA 94559. 707-253-7733. *Innkeeper:* Joanna Guidotti. Open all year.

Churchill Manor Inn is an 1889 mansion, which, with its many verandas and columns, resembles those of the antebellum South. Listed in the National Register, the mansion was built for a wealthy banker and vintner, Edward Churchill. High ceilings, brass and crystal chandeliers, and carved hardwoods complement Oriental carpets and formal Victorian furnishings. In addition to its lavish period furniture, each guest room offers something unique: A treadle sewing machine, Italian gold-laced tiling, or a Jacuzzi. The grandeur of the rooms allows for many special events — weddings and receptions or private wine tastings. The innkeeper will gladly arrange catered parties, dinners, or luncheons.

*Accommodations:* 8 rooms with private bath. *Pets, smoking, and children under 12:* Not permitted. *Driving Instructions:* As you enter Napa from Route 29, take the Imola exit to Jefferson. Turn left, continue 3/4 mile to Oak, turn right, and go 7 blocks and turn right at Brown. The inn is the first driveway.

## LA RESIDENCE COUNTRY INN

4066 Saint Helena Highway, Napa, CA 94558. 707-253-0337. *Innkeepers:* David R. Jackson and Craig E. Claussen. Open all year. La Residence Country Inn is a fine example of Victorian Gothic Revival architecture. The house, known locally as the "mansion," was built in 1870 by a river pilot from New Orleans who hit pay dirt in the California Gold Rush and settled in the wine country.

Now restored, the inn offers Victorian suites that have fireplaces, with more casual rooms on the third floor. On the grounds is "Cabernet Hall," built in the style of a French country barn, that has eleven suites furnished with English and French country-style pine antiques and Laura Ashley fabrics. All these rooms have fireplaces and French doors that open to a deck. A full breakfast is served in Hall House. In the evening, guests gather for a glass of wine and a relaxing soak in the Jacuzzi, if desired. There is a heated swimming pool on the grounds.

*Accommodations:* 20 rooms, 18 with private bath and fireplace. *Pets and smoking:* Not permitted. *Driving Instructions:* From Route 29, just north of Napa, pass through the Salvador Avenue intersection and turn right at the next road; follow the sign to the inn.

# THE OLD WORLD INN

1301 Jefferson Street, Napa, CA 94559. 707-257-0112. *Innkeepers:* Diane Dumaine. Open all year.

Built in 1906, the Old World Inn is an eclectic blend of architectural styles, mostly Victorian, with shingle siding, shaded porches, and diamond-pane windows.

What sets this inn apart from many other bed-and-breakfast establishments is its carefully orchestrated use of decorator papers and linens. Partly in tribute to designer Carl Larsson, who was starting to make his mark on the world of design when the inn was built, a selection of Home Port/China Seas fabrics and papers are used that have characteristically bright Swedish colors and that set off the Victorian and pre-Victorian antiques throughout the inn. Guest rooms are each uniquely decorated with canopy beds and most bathrooms have clawfooted tubs. The inn also has a large tiled, outdoor Jacuzzi for guests' use.

Breakfast is served in the Morning Room, where floral tablecloths and swagged valance curtains create a cheerful effect. Tea and homemade cookies are served each in the afternoons, and wine and cheese, along with a dessert buffet, in the evenings.

*Accommodations:* 8 rooms with private bath. *Pets, children, and smoking:* Not permitted. *Driving Instructions:* Take the Imola turnoff from Route 29 (at Napa). Turn right onto Imola and left onto Jefferson Street.

## GRANDMERE'S INN

449 Broad Street, Nevada City, CA 95959. 916-265-4660. *Innkeeper:* Annette Schaffer Meade. Open all year.

Grandmere's Inn was home to one of California's illustrious nineteenth-century families, the Sargents, Aaron Augustus and his wife, Ellen Clark. Aaron Sargent, a politician, championed the TransContinental Railroad and women's suffrage. As a U.S. Senator, he authored the 1878 bill known as The Anthony Amendment, which provided for women's voting rights. Ellen Clark Sargent was a pioneer suffragist and lifelong friend of Susan B. Anthony.

Today this three-story Colonial Revival home is listed in the National Register of Historic Places. Annette has decorated the 1856 house in a casual style, with light country-pine furniture, baskets, greenery, and bunches of dried and silk flowers. Handmade quilts and piles of floral patterned pillows decorate the beds and the living room sofas. A full breakfast is served in the dining room.

*Accommodations:* 6 rooms with private bath. *Pets and smoking:* Not permitted. *Children:* Under 14 restricted. *Driving Instructions:* Take Route 80 to Route 49 or Route 20 to Nevada City. Exit on Broad Street.

## NATIONAL HOTEL

211 Broad Street, Nevada City, CA 95959. 916-265-4551. *Innkeeper:* Thomas A. Coleman. Open all year.

The cupola of the National Hotel was a landmark to travelers when the hotel first opened in 1854, and it still beckons those approaching on the "Gold Country Highway'—Route 49. In fact, the National Hotel has never closed its doors, making it the oldest continuously operated hotel in California. In its early days, Nevada City was the "Queen of the Northern Mines," and the spirit of the bawdy Gold Rush days lives on in Victorian splendor in Tom Coleman's restoration.

The public rooms and guest rooms are decorated with Victorian antiques, period floral wallpapers, chandeliers, and velvet-and-satin love seats and chairs. The parlor–lounge has a square grand piano that was brought around the Horn on a schooner. An old clock with a giant pendulum still ticks in the corner.

Nine of the guest rooms have adjoining sitting rooms with velvet-cushioned love seats, marble-topped dressers, and end tables. All the rooms have period beds, some of which are large, canopied affairs with flower-print drapes, dust ruffles, and white crocheted spreads. Some of the guest rooms open onto the long veranda across the front of the hotel, overlooking an old-fashioned walkway below, where cocktails and lunch are served in the summer.

The cocktail lounge inside boasts a famous ornate bar, once the buffet in the Spreckels Mansion on San Francisco's Nob Hill. The dining room, open to the public for all three meals, has tables lighted by coal oil lamps and red glass chandeliers. The dinner menu offers many seafood dishes, as well as prime ribs and steaks. One of the modern amenities added for guests' enjoyment is a swimming pool just outside the hotel.

*Accommodations:* 43 guest rooms, 30 with private bath. *Pets:* Not permitted. *Driving Instructions:* Nevada City is 28 miles north of Auburn on Route 49. Take the Broad Street exit.

## RED CASTLE INN

109 Prospect Street, Nevada City, CA 95959. 916-265-5135. *Innkeepers:* Conley and Mary Louise Weaver. Open all year.

The Red Castle Inn is an extraordinary testimony to the gingerbread "baker's" art. Built in 1857, the four-story Gothic revival brick building has row after row of verandas and porches with elaborate balconies. The roof line and gables are decorated with a continuous row of carved wooden icicles to complete the "frosting" on the cake. The ef-

fect of all this is heightened by its position high on Prospect Hill overlooking the historic mining town of Nevada City.

The Red Castle Inn is old by Western standards and has managed to avoid the modernizing hand. The building has been changed very little since Judge John Williams built it as a castle symbolizing his wealth, amassed in gold strikes. The guest rooms are furnished with Victorian antiques. There is a comfortable parlor, complete with an 1880 pump organ. Paths to the town below lead through a series of terraced gardens, past a pond. A buffet breakfast and afternoon tea are served daily.

*Accommodations:* 8 rooms, 6 with private bath. *Pets and smoking:* Not permitted. *Children:* Under 10 not permitted. *Driving Instructions:* Nevada City is reached by the Gold Country Highway, Route 49. I-80 serves this general area.

## DORYMAN'S INN

2102 West Ocean Front, Newport Beach, CA 92663. 714-675-7300.
*Innkeeper:* Michael Sorrell. Open all year.

The original part of the Doryman's Inn, named in honor of the fishermen and the dory fishing fleet that ply the waters of the Pacific, was constructed in the 1920s as a boarding house for these men. Today, Doryman's has been completely reconstructed and redecorated. Guest rooms have skylights festooned with greenery, "flick-of-the-switch" fireplaces, sunken marble tubs, and gilded, beveled mirrors, some set in the headboards of luxurious canopied bedsteads. One guest room is a bower of red-and-white floral designs incorporated into the drapery, canopy, and dustruffle fabrics. Another room has lacy palms, stately Victorian antiques, and richly printed fabrics on a canopied four-poster bed. Amid these antique furnishings, guests find thoroughly modern amenities such as telephones in bedrooms and bathrooms, color-television sets, and king- and queen-size beds. Many rooms overlook the ocean, and the rest open onto the garden patio, where breakfast is served on clear, sunny mornings. On other days, breakfast is set out in the parlor.

*Accommodations:* 10 rooms with private bath. *Pets and children:* Not permitted. *Driving instructions:* Take Route 55 (the Newport Freeway) to Newport Boulevard and continue into Newport Beach. Turn right on 32nd Street, left on Balboa Boulevard, and bear right at the next light and drive to the Newport Pier area.

*North Hollywood, California*

## LA MAIDA HOUSE

11159 La Maida Street, North Hollywood, CA 91601. 818-769-3857.
*Innkeeper:* Megan Timothy. Open all year.

La Maida is an Old World–style villa built in the 1920s, a landmark estate set in a quiet residential neighborhood just minutes from Hollywood, Beverly Hills, and downtown Los Angeles. Surrounded by beautifully landscaped grounds with tall shade trees, fountains, and flower gardens, the villa is known locally as the "window house" because Megan Timothy created eighty-seven works in stained glass, including windows, skylights, and even a shower door. There are antiques and fresh cut flowers in all the rooms.

Each guest room is uniquely decorated. One, Cipresso, has a sitting area furnished with cushioned wicker set on a woven grass rug, as well as a canopied bed swagged with white drapes. The main feature of the Magnolia Room is a carved walnut Victorian bedroom set with a floral appliquéd quilt on the bed. Breakfast is served to guests either in the dining room or on the balcony. Among the amenities at La Maida are morning coffee or tea in bed and newspapers. Jacuzzis, a gazebo, a swimming pool, and a gym are available.

*Accommodations:* 7 rooms and 5 suites with private bath. *Pets and smoking:* Not permitted. *Driving Instructions:* Heading north on the Hollywood Freeway (170), exit at Magnolia Boulevard. Turn right and drive to the first light. Turn right on Tujunga Boulevard and proceed to the next light. Turn left on Camarillo and drive three blocks to Bellflower. Turn left and drive one block to the inn at the corner of Bellflower and La Maida Street.

## OJAI MANOR HOTEL

210 East Matilija, Ojai, CA 93023. 805-646-0961. *Innkeeper:* Mary
Nelson. Open all year.

The Ojai Manor Hotel is this town's oldest building, constructed as
its first schoolhouse in 1874. It is surrounded by gardens, lawns, and
tall white and live oaks and pepper trees. The inn has an eclectic decor
that blends old and new—one sees hand-crafted tables and a handmade
desk, Oriental rugs, and an overstuffed sofa and chair from the early
1900s. Innkeeper Mary Nelson has displayed her collection of folk art
and memorabilia in several rooms, and lavish bouquets of fresh flowers
are everywhere. There are twig tables and antique rag rugs in some guest
rooms, while European-style oversize feather pillows and bedside lamps
are added comforts. One room has Mission furniture and a lace coverlet
on its bed; another has antique fabrics and a brass bed topped with
a "crazy" quilt.

Breakfasts are served at a large hand-crafted table near the dining
room's wood-burning stove. The wraparound porch and balconies are
favorites with guests in the summer, and sherry and brandy are served
by the fireside in the living room during cooler weather.

*Accommodations:* 6 rooms with shared baths. *Smoking:* Not permitted. *Children:* Not permitted. *Driving instructions:* From Route 101,
take Route 33 fourteen miles to Ojai. Matilija Street is one block north
of Ojai Avenue.

*Pacific Grove, California*

## THE CENTRELLA

612 Central Avenue, Pacific Grove, CA 93950. 408-372-3372. *Innkeeper:* Elisa G. Frankel. Open all year.

The Centrella was built of redwood, about a century ago, as a boarding house. This three-story Victorian hotel and its five adjacent cottages were completely restored in 1982. Its designers have been given the Gold Key Award of the American Hotel and Motel Association for excellence in interior design.

The hotel is furnished and decorated with antiques. Laura Ashley textiles and wallpapers have been used effectively. Guest rooms are color-coordinated, and many of the private bathrooms still have claw-footed tubs. Five cottage suites have working fireplaces; two "honeymoon" suites have skylights. The dining room–parlor has a fireplace, around which guests may have evening sherry and hors d'oeuvres. A full breakfast is served buffet style in the dining room, overlooking the garden.

*Accommodations:* 26 rooms, 24 with private bath. *Pets:* Not permitted. *Smoking:* Restricted. *Driving Instructions:* From U.S. 1 take Route 68 west to Forest Ave.; continue on Forest to Central Avenue and turn left one block to the hotel.

## THE GOSBY HOUSE INN

643 Lighthouse Avenue, Pacific Grove, CA 93950. 408-375-1287.
*Innkeeper:* Kelly Short. Open all year.

Listed in the National Register of Historic Places, the Gosby House Inn is a Victorian mansion that was built in stages, beginning about 1886. During the early years, Mr. Gosby made it a practice to add something new on the house every winter. The Queen Anne tower that dominates the corner of the house today is one such addition.

Both the interior and exterior have been redone with care. Each room is furnished with antiques to create a Victorian atmosphere. In the parlor is an antique-doll collection. Many rooms have fireplaces; some have patios or porches; all have floral print wallpapers and chintz curtains. Throughout the mansion, the original stained glass and wooden moldings have been carefully preserved. A full buffet breakfast is served, as are wine and hors d'oeuvres.

Pacific Grove was originally a retreat from the more hectic life in the urban centers of California. Visitors today will find spectacular ocean vistas, Victorian homes, and a number of quality restaurants.

*Accommodations:* 22 guest rooms, 20 with private bath. *Pets and smoking:* Not permitted. *Driving Instructions:* Take Route 1 to the Pebble Beach–Pacific Grove turnoff. Turn right onto Route 68 West and follow the scenic route into Pacific Grove. Continue on Forest Avenue to Lighthouse Avenue, turn left, and go 3 blocks to the Inn.

## GREEN GABLES INN

104 Fifth Street, Pacific Grove, CA 93950. 408-375-2095. *Innkeeper:* Claudia Long. Open all year.

The Green Gables Inn is a fanciful 1888 Queen Anne house at the edge of Monterey Bay. Its guest rooms and two-room suite are furnished with antiques and decorated in soft colors. Fluffy quilts, tiny-floral-print wallpaper, and eaves, nooks, and crannies contribute to its old-fashioned atmosphere. Many rooms have fireplaces and views of the water. Breakfast is served in the dining room, where guests have a panoramic view of the bay. Guests can order gourmet picnics; after-noon tea is set out by the fireside in the living room, which contains a collection of antiques and has bay-windowed alcoves that overlook the sea. It's a short walk to the Monterey Bay Aquarium.

*Accommodations:* 11 rooms, 7 with private bath. *Pets:* Not per-mitted. *Smoking:* Carriage House only. *Driving Instructions:* From Route 1, take Route 68 west to Forest Street and Ocean View Boulevard at Fifth Street, overlooking the bay.

## SEVEN GABLES INN

555 Ocean View Boulevard, Pacific Grove, CA 93950. 408-372-4341.
*Innkeepers:* The Flatley family. Open all year.

Seven Gables Inn is a century-old Victorian mansion perched on a rocky promontory that juts into the Monterey Bay. The Flatley family renovated Seven Gables, filling it with their heirlooms and many other European and American antiques.

The personal family touches and the formal elegance of the antiques complement the comfortable upholstered pieces, crystal chandeliers, Oriental rugs, and fine detailing of the wood and plasterwork in this well-crafted home. And, of course, there are views of the California coastline from each guest room. One can relax in a guest-room easy chair or out on a flower-trimmed patio and watch sea otters, harbor seals, and whales pass in parade. At night the sounds of the sea lull guests to sleep. Guests are treated to ample breakfasts and, in the afternoon, to an elegant high tea. The inn is within minutes of Cannery Row, Monterey Bay Aquarium, Fisherman's Wharf, Carmel, and Big Sur.

*Accommodations:* 14 rooms with private bath. *Pets and smoking:* Not permitted. *Driving Instructions:* In Pacific Grove, take Forest Avenue to Ocean View Boulevard, turn right and drive two blocks to the inn.

## Palm Springs, California

## VILLA ROYALE INN

1620 Indian Trail, Palm Springs, CA 92264. 619-327-2314. *Innkeepers:* Robert E. Lee and C. Murawski. Open all year.

This Old-World–style inn has interior courtyards enclosed by Mediterranean tile-roofed villas and suites shaded with palm trees and cascading bougainvillea. There are fountains in the garden and an outdoor living room with a fireplace surrounded by wicker furniture. Two large swimming pools dot the inn's 3 1/2 acres. Many suites and rooms have private patios, spas, and working fireplaces, each decorated with antiques from a particular European country. Each evening there is a prix fixé dinner (again featuring the cuisine of a particular European country) with four to six à la carte entrées. A Continental breakfast is served and picnic lunches will be prepared by request.

*Accommodations:* 24 rooms with private bath. *Pets and children:* Not permitted. *Driving Instructions:* From East Palm Canyon Highway, in the center of Palm Springs, turn onto the Indian Trail. The inn is 1/2 block from TY ERROREast Palm Canyon Highway.

## Palo Alto, California

# THE VICTORIAN ON LYTTON

555 Lytton Avenue, Palo Alto, CA 94301. 415-322-8555. *Innkeepers:* Maxwell and Susan Hall. Open all year.

This blue-and-white Queen-Anne–style house was built in 1895 as a home for Hannah K. Clapp, a pioneer teacher and promoter of the women's suffrage movement. In 1859 Miss Clapp headed west, crossing the plains on horseback, wearing bloomers so she could ride astride her steed and toting a pistol. Following a career as a schoolteacher at the Sierra Academy, which she had founded in Carson City, Nevada, Miss Clapp retired to Palo Alto, sharing her home with two women students from Stanford University, one of whom occupied the house until 1936.

The house and English-style garden tidy. Tea or a glass of port is offered to arriving guests. Guest rooms are decorated and named for Queen Victoria or one of her children. Continental breakfasts are served in guests' rooms.

*Accommodations:* 10 rooms with private bath. *Pets and smoking:* Not permitted. *Children:* Under 16 not permitted. *Driving Instructions:* From Route 101 southbound, exit west on University Avenue. Turn right a Middlefield and left at Lytton.

*Placerville, California*

## CHICHESTER HOUSE BED AND BREAKFAST

800 Spring Street, Placerville, California. CA 95667. 916-626-1882.
*Innkeeper:* Nan Carson. Open all year.

Chichester House was built in 1892 by lumber baron D.W. Chichester. He spared no expense in creating "The Mansion" for his second wife, Caroline. Today, it is an inviting inn with a few surprises under its dining room. Below this room are two mine shaft entrances which, to this date, have been explored only by a few adventurous kittens who had to be coaxed out with tempting morsels. The old mine apparently was worked by Chinese laborers who camped on the hill behind.

Nan Carson, a trove of information about her inn and its history, has maintained the Victorian atmosphere of Chichester House through her use of antiques and family heirlooms. Grandmother Carson's rocker and oak pieces are in one guest room, and another displays a portion of wedding gown and other personal momentos. Each room has a private toilet and basin. Guests can relax in the parlor, with its old pump organ. The library is the another spot in which to relax and read or enjoy a game of cards. Nan serves a full breakfast in the dining room.

*Accommodations:* 3 rooms with half baths, all sharing 1 master bath. *Pets and smoking:* Not permitted. *Children:* Not permitted. *Driving instructions:* Take Spring Street 1/2 block north of Route 50.

## THE FLEMING JONES HOMESTEAD

3170 Newtown Road, Placerville, CA 95667. 916-626-5840. *Innkeeper:* Janice C. Condit. Open all year.

In the early 1880s, Florence Jones often complained to her husband, Fleming, that her house must be certain to burn up, so in need of repair was it. Fleming, who owned an interest in a bar in Grizzley Flat, was an ardent gambler. One evening he came home and placed a heap of money on the dining room table and said to his wife, "There, go build yourself a new house." The result, known today as the Fleming Jones Homestead, was sturdily built of entirely clear lumber — the best that gambling money could buy.

Once comprising 96 acres, The Homestead now consists of five buildings on 11 acres, including the farmhouse, an old red barn, a bunkhouse, and a milk house that has been transformed into the innkeeper's dwelling. The public and guest rooms are in the farmhouse and the rustic bunkhouse.

The Homestead's atmosphere is that of a warm, comfortable nineteenth-century farmhouse. Rooms are brightly decorated with antiques and relics from the last two centuries. Janice Condit makes award-winning jams, jellies, pickles, relishes and herbal and fruit vinegars, most of which appear on the table at breakfast and are avaiable for purchase.

The dining room's unusual oaken dining table has hand-carved griffins for legs and extends to 12 feet to accommodate guests. A Hoosier cabinet in this room has a built-in flour sifter, and a breakfront holds many of Janice's hand-painted china pieces and her crystal collection.

The parlor has a southern exposure and antique pieces, including an old church pump organ and a Morris rocker. One guest room is the Oak and Rose Room, which has an ornately carved oaken headboard and overlooks the rose garden and meadow. Upstairs, the Flower Basket Room has a restored ivory iron bed. The largest room, Lover's Fancy, has an iron-and-brass bedstead and catches the morning sun.

The meadows and woods around the Fleming Jones Homestead make it a peaceful refuge from which to explore the surrounding Gold Rush area and its emerging wine industry, as well as nearby Lake Tahoe. Old burros, a Welsh pony, a Shetland pony, and some ducks and chickens add to the pastoral atmosphere of the setting.

*Accommodations:* 6 rooms with private bath. *Pets:* Not permitted. *Children:* Under 12 discouraged for safety. *Driving Instructions:* The Homestead is east of Placerville, 1 1/2 miles south of I-50 on Newtown Road.

## Point Reyes Station, California

## HOLLY TREE INN

    3 Silverhills Road, Point Reyes Station, California. Mailing address: Box 642, Point Reyes Station, CA 94956. 415-663-1554. *Innkeepers:* Diane and Tom Balogh. Open all year except Christmas.

Holly Tree nestles at the foot of a mountain, just a mile from the headquarters of Point Reyes National Seashore, one of the most beautiful stretches of rugged coastline in the world. The inn's secluded 19 country acres provide a pleasant haven of old English boxwood, lilacs, and an arbor of manicured holly trees.

    The guest rooms and public rooms are on the second floor. The inn's centerpiece is a large airy living room decorated with antique quilts. The room opens onto a sunny porch where pots of petunias and pansies line the railings and old-fashioned rockers and a porch swing await guests. The living and dining rooms have working fireplaces. Overstuffed couches and chairs are grouped in front of the brick hearth, a favorite spot for enjoying an afternoon glass of wine. A country-style breakfast is served each morning by the dining room's curved hearth.

    Guest rooms occupy the four bright corners of the house. The walls, drapes, and quilts are Laura Ashley prints. The Ivy Room, with its spool bed and white ruffled curtains, looks out through an ivy-covered lattice to the hillside.

    *Accommodations:* 4 rooms with private bath; 2 cottages. *Pets:* Not permitted. *Smoking:* Restricted. *Driving Instructions:* From Olema, take Route 1 North. Take the first left onto Bear Valley Road, then look for the Holly Tree sign, third left turn after park headquarters.

## THE FEATHER BED

542 Jackson Street, Quincy, California. Mailing address: P.O. Box 3200, Quincy, CA 95971. 916-283-0102. *Innkeepers:* Chuck and Dianna Goubert. Open all year.

Quincy is a small mountain town in the heart of the Northern Sierra's "Feather River Country," an area steeped in gold-mining history. The Feather Bed Inn is a peach-colored Victorian built in 1893 with a Greco-Roman facade added at the turn of the century. Dianna and Chuck Goubert have restored the house, decorating it with country Victorian antiques and wallpapers. The formal parlor is a favorite spot in the early evening. Breakfast is served in the dining room, on the brick courtyard, or in guests' rooms, each of which has something special: a private balcony overlooking Quincy, a separate sitting room, or a view of the mountains. Guests here can enjoy Nordic skiing, antiquing, and the spectacular scenery. The Gouberts provide bicycles for touring the surrounding countryside, which encompasses lakes, rivers, meadows, tall timber, and mountain trails.

*Accommodations:* 7 rooms with private bath. *Pets, smoking and children:* Not permitted. *Driving Instructions:* Take Route 70-89 to Quincy, northwest of Reno. Route 70-89 is Quincy's Main Street. Jackson Street is one block south of Main Street.

## CHRISTMAS HOUSE BED & BREAKFAST INN

9240 Archibald Avenue, Rancho Cucamonga, CA 91730. 714-980-6450. *Owner:* Janice Ilsley. *Innkeeper:* Zannell Blahut. Open all year.

Christmas House, a Queen Anne Victorian built at the turn of the century, has landscaped grounds dotted with tall palm trees. Its name stems from its red and green stained-glass windows and from an early owner's penchant for throwing elaborate parties, especially at Christmas. The current innkeepers continue the tradition.

The inn is furnished with Victorian antiques. There are two parlors and a library, seven working fireplaces, stained-glass windows, and ornate carved woodwork. Celebration Suite, with its canopy bed draped with antique lace, has two working hearths, one in the bedroom and one in the parlor. Vineyard Room is decorated in a French country style, while Cabernet Room has rich wine colors, a crystal chandelier, and walnut antiques.

Breakfast is treated as a special occasion, one where a guest might find sweet cheese crêpes or a hot spiced fruit compote. The inn is less than an hour from southern California's varied activities and sights. Hiking trails and downhill skiing and are with fifteen miles.

*Accommodations:* 5 rooms, 2 with private bath. *Pets and smoking:* Not permitted. *Children:* Under 13 not permitted. *Driving Instructions:* From I-10, take the Archibald Avenue exit in Cucamonga and go north 1 1/4 miles to the inn. Cucamonga is 40 miles east of Los Angeles.

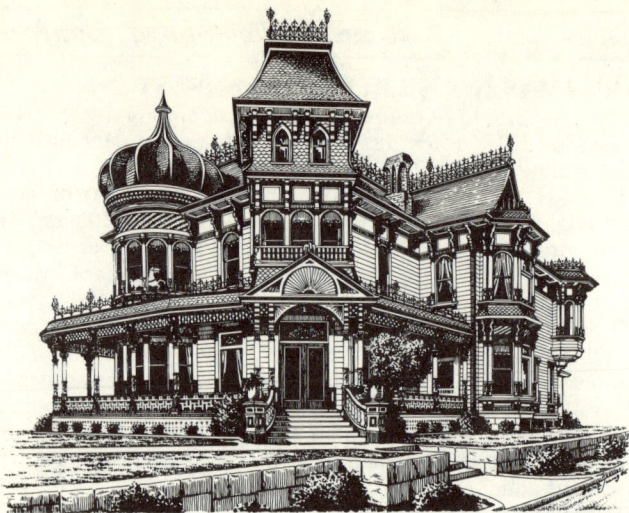

*Redlands, California*

## MOREY MANSION

190 Terracina Boulevard, Redlands, CA 92373. 714-793-7970. *Innkeeper:* Stephen Cushman. Open all year.

Morey Mansion, a valentine to pure Victoriana, is possibly the most famous house in the area. It has been featured in everything from movies and television shows to cartoons and greeting cards. Its architecture includes Gothic arched windows, Italianate balustrades, a Chinese traceried veranda, and a Saracenic onion dome. The interior incorporates intricately carved golden oak, carved serpent tails which twine around stair railings, and orange blossoms carved into door and window trim. Each of the lavish Victorian rooms has an alcove; four in the library alone. Overnight guests have the use of the parlors and music room. Teas, wine, and sherry are set out in early evening, accompanied by savories. Breakfast is served in the dining room in or on the porch.

*Accommodations: 6 rooms, 2 with private bath. Pets and children:* Not permitted. *Driving Instructions:* From Interstate 10 take the Alabama exit south, follow the "H" (hospital) signs 2.6 miles to Terracina and Olive Ave.

## AMBER HOUSE BED AND BREAKFAST

1315 Twenty-second Street, Sacramento, CA 95816. 916-444-8085.

*Innkeepers:* Jane and Michael Richardson. Open all year.

The brick stairway of Amber House, a 1905 Arts and Crafts-style bungalow, is flanked by flower boxes and leads to the entrance porch and distinctive beveled-glass inset front door. The living room has a box-beamed ceiling of natural alder wood, Oriental rugs, and bookshelves that flank the brick fireplace. Baskets of fruits and nuts are set out in the guest rooms, and a decanter of sherry is always available in the library. Breakfast is served in the formal dining room, which has stained-glass windows, or in guests' own rooms.

Guest rooms have private telephones, televisions, cassette players, air-conditioning, and private baths. Lindworth has stained-glass windows, a skylight, and an antique bathtub. Wicklow has Delft-blue wallpaper and beveled- and stained-glass windows. A tandem bicycle is available for pedaling to the Capitol, Old Sacramento and nearby attractions.

*Accommodations:* 5 rooms with private bath. *Pets and smoking:* Not permitted. *Children:* Under 12 not permitted. *Driving Instructions:* The inn is seven blocks east of the State Capitol, between Capitol and N Streets.

## THE BRIGGS HOUSE

2209 Capitol Avenue, Sacramento, CA 95816. 916-441-3214. *Owner:* Susan Selbin. *Innkeepers:* Pam Giordano. Open all year.

In 1981, several partners opened Sacramento's first bed-and-breakfast inn. Their creation, The Briggs House, is a booming successs thanks to a combination of antique furnishings in an atmosphere of informal elegance, thoughtful attention to such details as beverages and fruit awaiting guests, and decorative touches provided by family heirlooms.

The Briggs House was built in 1901 for a prominent physician. Shady lawns, a sauna, and an old-fashioned veranda invite guests to settle in and relax.

Each spacious room at the inn has its own special feature — Sunrise Suite has a sun deck, the Fireside Room has a fireplace, and others have brass or elaborate oaken beds, Oriental rugs, and lacy pillows. Sleepy Hollow, in the Carriage House, has a fireplace and a claw-footed tub. A sitting room and library are the public rooms. Full breakfasts are served to guests.

*Accommodations:* 3 rooms with shared bath; 4 with private bath. *Pets, smoking, and children under 10:* Not permitted. *Driving Instructions:* The inn is on Capitol Avenue, seven blocks east of the capitol.

## DRIVER MANSION INN

2019 21st Street, Sacramento, CA 95818. 916-455-5243. *Innkeepers:* Sandra and Richard Kann. Open all year.

Driver Mansion, an impeccably restored Victorian built in 1899 for a prominent Sacramento attorney, Philip Driver, and his family, is an example of Colonial Revival architecture that escaped the ravages and modernizations of time by remaining in the Driver family until 1977. Today, it is a lavish bed-and-breakfast inn, furnished in rich, subdued colors, with mahogany and walnut antiques and plush wall-to-wall carpeting. A 1907 Chickering grand piano is the centerpiece of the parlor, which has leaded-glass windows and an elaborate fireplace. Bathrooms have Jacuzzis and turn-of-the-century fixtures; guest rooms have scrolly brass-and-iron beds, fireplaces, and skylights. A penthouse suite has a black marble bathroom, a sitting room and a bedroom. Rooms in the Carriage House have a Jacuzzi and a marble fireplace. Guests start their day with breakfast in the dining room or in the garden.

*Accommodations:* 8 rooms with private bath. *Pets and smoking:* Not permitted. *Driving instructions:* From I-80, take the 15th Street exit and drive east to 21st Street.

## HOTEL ST. HELENA

1309 Main Street, Saint Helena, CA 94574. 707-963-4388. *Innkeepers:* Athena Martin and Mary Martin. Open all year.

Hotel St. Helena is in its second century of serving travelers. Victorian antiques blend with wall-to-wall carpeting, air-conditioning, and plush love seats. The color scheme of rich burgundies, mauves, chocolate browns, and tans is picked up in the floral-and-stripe pattern of the halls. Continental breakfasts feature blueberry muffins and scones, along with fresh fruit and beverages. In winter everyone gathers by the fireside in the lobby for breakfast or an afternoon drink at the bar.

There is a sitting room at the top of the stairs, and a second-story veranda overlooks the arcade behind the hotel. All guest rooms are decorated with quilted spreads and dust ruffles on queen-size or twin brass, painted iron, or carved wooden beds. Each room has at least

one antique piece, and all windows have white shutters.

*Accommodations:* 18 rooms, 14 with private bath. *Pets, smoking, and children:* Not permitted. *Driving Instructions:* Take Route 29 to Saint Helena.

## THE INK HOUSE

1575 St. Helena Highway, St. Helena, CA 94574. 707-963-3890. *Innkeepers:* Lois and George Clark. Open all year.

Ink House is an Italianate-Victorian farmhouse in the heart of the Napa Valley. Built in 1884 for Theron H. Ink on 1 1/2 acres surrounded by vineyards, the inn is listed in the National Register of Historic Places. Lois and George moved here in 1947 and raised five children in their home before transforming it, in 1977, into a bed-and-breakfast inn. An observatory with stained-glass windows, originally Mr. Ink's treetop office, offers a panoramic view of the surrounding vineyards and hills. Downstairs, the parlor is furnished with antiques and has a fireplace and an old-fashioned pump organ. Four bedrooms have lace curtains and handmade quilts on antique beds. A Continental breakfast of homemade nutbreads and muffins is served in the dining room.

*Accommodations:* 4 rooms with private bath. *Pets, smoking, and children:* Not permitted. *Driving Instructions:* The inn is on Route 29, south of St. Helena, at the southwest corner of Whitehall Lane.

This book cannot possibly detail the many tourist attractions in a city the size of San Diego, but visitors may want to consider a stop at *Balboa Park,* with its many museums, including the *Fleet Space Theater, Natural History Museum, San Diego Zoo, Timken Art Gallery, Fine Arts Gallery,* and *San Diego Hall of Champions.* Other important San Diego attractions are *Sea World*, the *Maritime Museum*, and *Mission San Diego*. For tourist information, see our companion *Guide to California and the Pacific Northwest* or stop at the San Diego Convention and Visitors Bureau at 1200 Third Avenue, Suite 824. 714-232-3101.

## BRITT HOUSE

406 Maple Street, San Diego, CA 92103. 619-234-2926. *Innkeepers:* Daun Martin. Open all year.

Britt House was built in 1887 by the influential California attorney Eugene Britt for a mere $3,000. Even accounting for the change in buying power over the last century, you will find this hard to believe as you enter the restored, turreted house. You are immediately greeted by one of the building's most distinctive features, its elaborate winding stairway backed by a series of stained-glass windows, which project pretty patterns on the nearby walls from the late afternoon sunlight. The inn, a testimony to the craftsmanship of a bygone era, has carved oak trim and fretwork, sliding doors that still operate after a century of use, detailed brass hinges, and decorative doorknobs. Britt House remained in good hands in its early years; after it was completed, Britt sold it to the Scripps family, which used it as a townhouse. Later it was a boardinghouse, a tearoom, a chiropractor's office, and then the domain of a local diet doctor. The neighborhood surrounding Britt House has been receiving recent attention because of its Victorian homes. At least six have been restored with a four-block area. The Maple Street location is only a block and a half from Balboa Park with its choice museums and family attractions.

The inn's guest rooms, divided between the first and second floors, have polished hardwood floors, a selection of Victorian antiques, and are decorated with inviting wallpapers, chosen with the tastes of the Victorian era in mind. The resulting prints, in hues of rust, pumpkin, peach, and blue, capture the Victorian flavor.

Individual touches at Britt House are its hallmark. The Governor's Room contains furniture that belonged to Robert Waterman, California's seventeenth governor. The Windsor Room features a canopy draped in velvets of burgundy, cerise, and crimson. Home-baked cookies, fresh fruit, and foil-wrapped candy kisses greet guests in every room. One bathroom has two bathtubs, allowing a couple to bathe together while maintaining the proper Victorian distance.

Guests are invited to formal tea in the parlor at 4 P.M. Breakfast includes juice, eggs, and freshly baked breads served in the guest rooms. One can look down from the balconies at the English gardens and the century-old camphor tree surrounded by the cyclamens, ferns, and azaleas of the inn's formal garden.

*Accommodations:* 10 rooms, 1 with private bath. *Pets and smoking:* Not permitted. *Driving Instructions:* From I-5, take the airport exit onto Kettner Boulevard. Go about a mile, then turn left at Laurel, again at Fifth, and a third time at Maple Street.

## HERITAGE PARK BED & BREAKFAST INN

2470 Heritage Park Row, San Diego, CA 92110. 619-295-7088. *Innkeeper:* Lori Chandler. Open all year.

This splendid Queen Anne mansion is with a peaceful eight-acre historical park in the heart of the city's Old Town, noted for buildings that date back to San Diego's Mexican and early-California periods. The turreted mansion is just one of seven nineteenth-century buildings in the park. It's nine guest rooms have wallpapers that are authentically documented from the Museum of American Folk Art, fainting couches, oversize claw-footed tubs, canopied and brass-and-iron beds, and carved and paneled antique furniture. The Victorian Rose Room has views of a private garden; the Turret Room is a honeymooner's haven with its Renaissance bed, private sitting room, and surrounding view of the city. In the evening guests enjoy a social hour in the parlor, where, later, classic old-time films are shown. Guests choose the spot for their full breakfast — a secluded corner of the wrap-around veranda or their own bed. A 5-course candlelit dinner served in one's own room can be arranged. The staff will gladly assist guests planning outings to the nearby San Diego Zoo, arrange boat tours of the bay, or engage a bicycle taxi to take guests on tours of Old Town and Presidio Park.

*Accommodations:* 9 rooms, 5 with private bath. *Pets, smoking, and children:* Not permitted. *Driving instructions:* Take I-5 to the Old Town Avenue exit. Turn left onto Old Town Avenue, left again on San Diego, right on Harney, and follow Harney to Heritage Park and the inn.

## THE ALBION HOUSE INN

135 Gough Street, San Francisco, CA 94102. 415-621-0896. *Innkeeper:* Jan Robert de Gier. Open all year.

Past residents of Albion House, which was built as temporary housing just after the great earthquake in 1906, would be more than a little surprised at the new look the hotel has taken on. Once through its beveledglass entranceway, one realizes that a transformation has occurred.

A hallway leading to the impeccable guest rooms upstairs is papered with a bird-of-paradise wall covering. The parlor has been totally redone with redwood beams, polished dark-wood floors, and colorful upholstered couches and chairs. This spacious living–dining room has a working fireplace, and guests frequently gather here before meals for a glass of sherry. Guest rooms have polished brass chandeliers, antique chests and armoires, and brass beds. English hunting scenes decorate the walls. There is even a greenhouse where orchids are grown. Charpe's, a restaurant that occupies the ground floor, is open to the public for dinner and Sunday brunch. The inn is located near theaters, the opera, museums, and restaurants.

*Accommodations:* 8 rooms with private bath. *Pets:* Not permitted. *Driving Instructions:* The hotel is on Gough Street between Oak and Page streets. Off-street parking available.

## THE ARCHBISHOPS MANSION

1000 Fulton Street, San Francisco, CA 94117. 415-563-7872. *Innkeepers:* Jonathan Shannon and Jeffrey Ross. Open all year.

The lavish restoration and decoration of The Archbishops Mansion merits only superlatives, having undergone two-and-a-half years of effort by Jonathan Shannon, who also restored The Spreckles Mansion. The Second Empire–style home of the archbishops of San Francisco for more than forty years, the 25,000-square-foot building is one of the three largest homes in the city. Constructed in 1904, it survived the San Francisco earthquake two years later. In 1934 the mansion was the overnight stopping place for the Pope.

In redoing the mansion, Jonathan chose the French-Victorian "Belle Epoque" style, which pays homage to the earlier Louis XV and XVI styles with heavy bronze chandeliers, rich draperies, gilt-framed pain-

tings, hand-carved mahogany columns and mantelpieces, and 12-foot pier mirrors. A 16-foot stained-glass dome lights a three-story open staircase. Carved beds are in all fourteen guest rooms, each named after a nineteenth-century opera. Ten rooms have fireplaces; in Carmen Suite, a claw-footed tub is set before the hearth. La Traviata Suite has a coffered ceiling, chandeliers, and a carved and canopied bed. One may soak in the double Jacuzzi in the Rosenkavalier Suite, a pair of rooms where rose and silver set the mood and French antiques are the rule. Overnight accommodations include breakfast, evening wine, and parking.

*Accommodations:* 15 rooms with private bath. *Pets:* Not permitted. *Driving Instructions:* The Mansion is on Fulton Street at Steiner, in the Alamo Square Historic District, six blocks west of the Opera House and Civic Center.

# THE BED AND BREAKFAST INN

4 Charlton Court, San Francisco, CA 94123. 415-921-9784. *Innkeepers:* Robert and Marily Kavanaugh. Open all year.

The Bed and Breakfast Inn is an English-style pension in the heart of San Francisco. Bob and Marily spent hundreds of hours carefully restoring the Victorian buildings, which now contain rooms for overnight guests with a touch of European service in the middle of a modern, bustling city. When the Kavanaughs opened their doors in 1976, they offered five rooms in their home on Charlton Court, an English-mews–style street. The success of the original inn enabled them to open an annex next door that now offers four luxurious additional rooms. One has a bath with a sunken double tub. Both buildings were constructed in the late nineteenth century and predate the disastrous earthquake of 1906.

The guest rooms greet new arrivals with fresh fruit and flowers, and there are books and magazines in abundance. Some of the rooms open onto a garden courtyard. In each the guest may snuggle into a sea of quilts and down pillows. The mews totally isolates the guest from city noises. The Kavanaughs have recently converted what was once their private flat into the Mayfair guest suite. The special accommodations include a latticed balcony, living room, kitchen, and spiral staircase to a bedroom-loft.

The only meal served is a Continental breakfast featuring croissants,

freshly baked coffee cake, and coffee or tea. Guests are welcome to have breakfast in bed on trays set with Wedgwood china, linen napkins, and fresh flowers. Flowers here are, in fact, the keynote, and guests are welcome in the garden.

*Accommodations:* 10 rooms, 5 with private bath. *Pets:* Not permitted. *Children:* Under 6 not permitted. *Driving Instructions:* The inn is on Charlton Court, a small street off Union between Laguna and Buchanan streets.

## EDWARD II INN

3155 Scott Street, San Francisco, CA 94123. 415-922-3000. *Innkeepers:* Bob and Denise Holland. Open all year.

Edward II is a European-style inn decorated with an English country flair. Accommodations include both rooms and suites. Some suites are in the inn, while others are in a Victorian carriage house across the street. Some suites have canopy beds, others have mirrored headboards. All have a wet bar and some have whirlpool baths. The Carriage House suites share a private garden, and each has its own living room and kitchen. Guest rooms have wicker dressers and quilts and dust ruffles on the beds.

Guests are served a Continental breakfast in the tile-floored Italian bakery that shares first-floor space with the hotel, the Marina Cafe Restaurant and Bloomer's Pub, where complimentary sherry is served nightly. A stained-glass skylight, garden lattice, and floral wall coverings set the mood.

*Accommodations:* 23 rooms, 14 with private bath; 6 suites. *Pets:* Not permitted. *Driving Instructions:* The hotel is in the marina district, 10 blocks west of Van Ness, at the corner of Lombard and Scott streets.

## HERMITAGE HOUSE
2224 Sacramento Street, San Francisco, CA 94115. 415-921-5515. *Innkeepers:* Robert C. Pritikin. Open all year.

Hermitage House is a seventeen-room Greek Revival home built between 1900 and 1903 for Judge Charles Slack by architect William Blaisdell. The entryway shows off the carved heart-redwood detailing typical of the period in the house's pillars, beams, and stairway scrolls. The many redwood mantels include those on the five working fireplaces in guest rooms.

The inn's extensive buffet breakfast is served on a handmade inlaid mahogany Williamsburg Colonial table and matching buffet and dropleaf serving table. A small alcove to the right of the entry was used in earlier days as a chapel for weddings, christenings, and funerals. The inn, with its garden, is a popular wedding location.

Each guest room is individually done. The three largest have comfortable sitting areas and working fireplaces, and one is done with redwood from its beams to its bookcase walls. There is a small, sunny porch on the top floor.

*Accommodations:* 5 rooms (some convertible to suites) with private bath. *Children:* Under 4 not permitted. *Driving Instructions:* From the south, take U.S. 101 to the Golden Gate exit, then drive up Franklin Street about twelve blocks toward the bay to Sacramento Street. Turn left on Sacramento to the inn. Off-street parking is available.

## THE INN SAN FRANCISCO

943 South Van Ness, San Francisco, CA 94110. 415-641-0188. *Innkeeper:* Joel Daily. Open all year.

The Inn San Francisco is an Italianate on "Mansion Row," San Francisco's historic Victorian district, now a working-class neighborhood ideally located near many of the city's attractions. The mansion was built in the 1870s for John English and his wife and seven children. Today its twenty-seven-rooms are lavishly furnished with antiques of the period, while fresh floral bouquets and soft classical music set the mood. There are still the original ornate woodwork, marble fireplaces, and etched- and stained-glass windows, all on a scale appropriate to the 14-foot-high ceilings. Lace-curtained guest rooms, decorated with formal Victorian antiques, have marble sinks, color-television sets, telephones, and refrigerators. Deluxe suites have their own spas, and some have fireplaces and private balconies. After enjoying the hot tub in the Victorian-style gazebo in the garden, guests can relax on the roof sundeck, which has panoramic views of the city. A breakfast buffet is served

in the antique-filled double parlor or in the garden. There is 24-hour service at the front desk.

*Accommodations:* 15 rooms, 13 with private bath. *Pets:* Not permitted. *Smoking:* Not in parlor. *Driving Instructions:* From the freeway (101) going north, take the Army Street exit west to South Van Ness.

## THE MANSION HOTEL

2220 Sacramento Street, San Francisco, CA 94115. 415-929-9444. *Owner:* Robert C. Pritikin. *Manager:* Denise Mitioieri. Open all year.

This is not an ordinary hotel. The macaw has just bitten a hunk out of the grand piano. People dine before a mural that stretches over several walls and bears the title *Pig-nic*.

The saga of the Mansion began years ago when Bob Pritikin heard it was for sale. The place was littered with sleeping hulks of some of San Francisco's hippies, but Pritikin saw past the debris and bought the place. He tossed the hippies out and stepped back to discover he was suddenly in possession of a hotel in the city's high-rent district. His inaugural ball, so to speak, came two weeks later, when he gave a party. To get ready for the party he dashed about from antique shop to antique wholesaler buying truckloads of whimsy, mostly from the Victorian era. Pritikin was content to leave no corner empty; the hotel spills over with treasures both real and fanciful. Mannequins in gowns that grandmother must have worn greet you in the grand foyer, a beaded purse collection hangs on one wall, reclaimed from a former spouse.

Hotel guests can partake of the fun at the Magic Concert, complete with a nightly guaranteed appearance of Claudia, the mansion hauntress. Bob Pritikin emerges from the wings to entertain one and all with his musical saw Friday and Saturday evenings at 7:00.

The Mansion is a grand old home built in 1887 by a Senator Chambers, who had amassed a fortune from a profitable mining business. He was sheriff for a while and reputedly presided over the first double hanging in the state. His niece Claudia is the ghost believed to haunt the Mansion. Behind the generous measure of fun at the Mansion is a first-class hotel that has truly fine, comfortable furnishings, mostly Victorian. The paneling that graces many walls could scarcely be replaced at any price. There are fresh flowers and a raft of unusual accessories in each room. The hotel's art collection is valued in the millions. Some of the murals on the walls portray several distinguished San Franciscans. The remainder run heavily to pigs and unicorns and other mythological creatures. The hotel's register has begun to read like a "Who's Who" of the West Coast.

Claudia's dining room is available to guests who wish to dine in the hotel, and room service is available from 7 A.M. to midnight.

*Accommodations:* 19 rooms with private bath. *Driving Instructions:* The hotel is four blocks west of Van Ness on Sacramento. It is 5 blocks from the California Street cable car stop.


## THE MONTE CRISTO

600 Presidio Avenue, San Francisco, CA 94115. 415-931-1875. *Innkeepers:* George Yuan. Open all year.

Exciting times have been had at the Monte Cristo. Built in 1875, it has served as a saloon, a bordello, a refuge for the injured after the 1906 earthquake, and a speakeasy. Completely restored in 1980, it now welcomes guests as an English-style urban bed-and-breakfast inn. When you arrive at The Monte Cristo you are welcomed, shown to your room, and offered a libation in the parlor, before a wood-burning fireplace. If it is late afternoon, you may pause to enjoy the hot English tea that is served.

The Monte Cristo's guest rooms have been done with style and grace. There are several Victorian rooms, a Georgian Room with canopied four-poster bed—popular with newlyweds—and an Oriental Room complete with a Chinese wedding bed and sunken tub. The Monte Cristo, two blocks from Sacramento Street and its popular shops and restaurants, is a ten-minute cab ride from the downtown business district.

*Accommodations:* 15 rooms, 12 with private bath. *Pets and children:* Not permitted. *Driving Instructions:* Take U.S. 101 to the Franklin Street exit. Drive to Pine Street; take Pine to Presidio Ave.

## PETITE AUBERGE

863 Bush Street, San Francisco, CA 94108. 415-928-6000. *Innkeeper:* Carolyn Vaughan. Open all year.

The facade of this intimate city hotel has a baroque design typical of many San Francisco buildings constructed in the early 1900s. Flower-

filled window boxes flank the bowed bay windows on each of the three floors.

Owners Roger and Sally Post transformed the hotel into a bed-and-breakfast inn with French country flair. Fresh bouquets of flowers, French country antiques, working fireplaces, and delicate French floral-print wallpapers all work to create an unusual setting. The lounge is appointed with polished antiques and groupings of sofas and chairs around the hearth. The only meals served, breakfast and afternoon tea and hors d'oeuvres, are set out for guests in the dining area. The guest rooms are decorated in soft colors with quilted bedspreads and handmade pillows. Each has a working fireplace, two fluffy robes, apples, a morning newspaper, and turn-down service. The Petite Auberge is just a few blocks from Nob Hill and the theater district.

*Accommodations:* 26 rooms with private bath. *Pets:* Not permitted. *Smoking:* Not permitted in public rooms. *Driving Instructions:* The hotel is in downtown San Francisco, 2 1/2 blocks from Union Square and two blocks from Nob Hill.

## THE QUEEN ANNE

1590 Sutter Street, San Francisco, CA 94109. 415-441-2828 (California) or 800-227-3970. *Innkeeper:* George Wright. Open all year.

The building that is now the Queen Anne once served as an exclusive men's club and a residential lodge. Now almost a century has passed, and The Queen Anne has been given a painstaking restoration (at a cost of almost $1.5 million) and has reopened as one of the city's most elegant small hotels. This landmark restoration is now included in many of the city's heritage tours.

A carved wooden staircase, lighted from above by a stained-glass skylight, sets the mood of Victorian elegance here. The intricate paneling and floor marquetry are perfect foils for tall, lacy palms, bouquets of fresh flowers, and fine English and American antiques. Guests are served afternoon tea and sherry by the fireside in the main parlor with its camelback settees and side chairs upholstered in rich brocades and deep red velvets.

There are bay windows, working fireplaces, and even marble wet bars in many of the guest rooms, which are decorated with Victorian antiques but also have modern baths, color television, paging systems, and numerous room services.

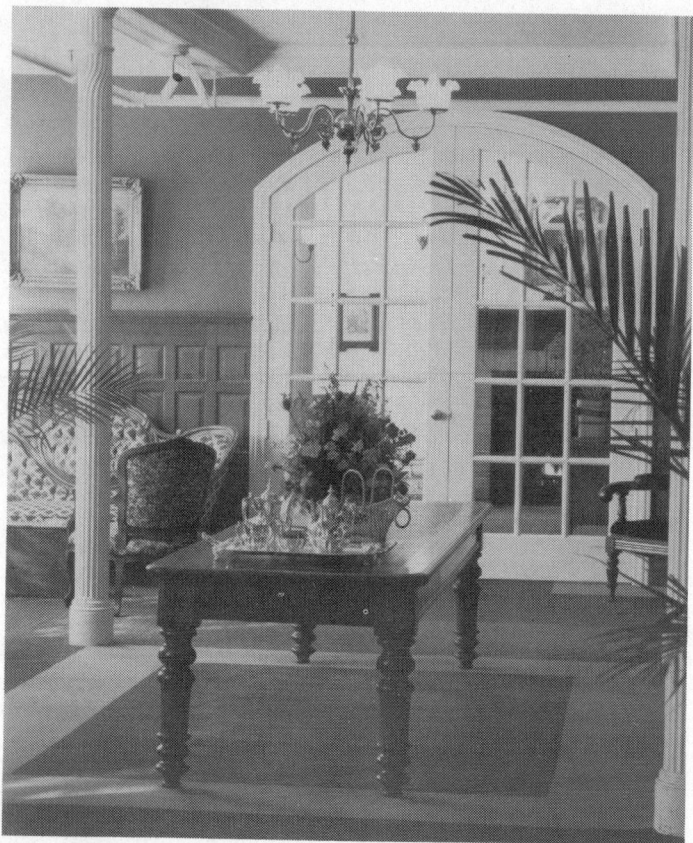

*Accommodations:* 49 rooms with private bath. *Pets:* Not permitted. *Driving Instructions:* The hotel is on Sutter Street at Octavia.

*San Francisco, California*

## THE SPRECKELS MANSION

737 Buena Vista West, San Francisco, CA 94117. 415-861-3008. *Innkeepers:* Jonathan Shannon and Kathleen Austin. Open all year.

The Spreckels family made its fortune in sugar and spent it well, building an elegant mansion high on Buena Vista Hill in 1887. The family would surely approve of the style with which Jonathan Shannon and Kathleen Austin have established their bed-and-breakfast inn. Once the home of Jack London and Ambrose Bierce, the mansion has been host to the likes of Gertrude Stein and Enrico Caruso.

The Spreckels Mansion is filled with the kinds of details that distinguish a stay at a small townhouse inn. There are original period chandeliers, several fireplaces (each different), a cushioned window seat for reading the library's many books, queen-size brass beds, marble sinks, and (in one bathroom) a free-standing tub in front of a fireplace. There are also stained-glass windows, abundant antiques, and more. Complimentary wine is offered in the library in the late afternoon, and a Continental breakfast is served every morning. If you are in the mood and have taken the Sugar Baron Suite, you can have your breakfast on a little balcony overlooking the park.

*Accommodations:* 10 rooms, 9 with private bath and 8 with fireplaces. *Pets:* Not permitted. *Driving Instructions:* Take Masonic Street to Frederic Street, and turn left on Buena Vista West.

## UNION STREET INN

    2229 Union Street, San Francisco, CA 94123. 415-346-0424. *Innkeeper:* Helen Stewart. Open all year.

Before the turn of the century, the Union Street section of San Francisco was known as "Cow Hollow" because of its acres of pasture land. The building boom in the early 1890s ended farming with the city, and today Union Street is a thriving section with many interesting shops and fine restaurants. Built in 1902, the Union Street Inn began its life as an elegant city home and was converted to a bed-and-breakfast inn, owned and operated by Helen Stewart, a former teacher.

The light-brown clapboard house has two floors of bay windows and a small columned front porch. The inn truly excels in the warmth and dignity of its rooms, where fine antiques representing the period combine with richly colored wallpapers, wall fabrics, carpeting, and polished hardwood floors. The small parlor, a popular gathering place, has a pair of unusual brass and leather Edwardian-period Australian chairs, an upholstered love seat, salmon-colored velvet wall coverings, a gas-log fireplace, and glass doors that open onto the sundeck. In all but the coolest months, the deck is a quiet spot to enjoy late afternoon wine and cheese. Just steps beyond is the English-style garden with brick walks and a profusion of carefully tended shrubs and flowers. The Carriage House, complete with guest room, big bay window, and Jacuzzi, is at the edge of the garden.

Honeymoon couples and garden lovers are encouraged to stay in the English Garden Room with its pearl gray and persimmon decor, patterned wall coverings, and Dutch door opening onto the garden. Another downstairs guest room is noted for its large and elegant armoire and canopied bed. The upstairs rooms also have marble sinks with each room and a table that may be used for breakfast unless guests prefer to eat in the parlor, on the deck, or to have breakfast in bed. The Continental breakfast includes freshly squeezed orange juice, hot coffee or tea, Helen's homemade jam, croissants, and muffins made by the same baker who supplies the French embassy. The Union Street Inn is a place where you are likely to linger awhile, and to which you are certain to return.

*Accommodations:* 5 rooms with private bath, and Carriage House. *Pets:* Not permitted. *Children:* Under 8 not permitted. *Driving Instructions:* Exit off the freeway (U.S. 101) at Franklin or Van Ness. Take either to Union Street and turn left to the inn.

## VICTORIAN INN ON THE PARK

301 Lyon Street, San Francisco, CA 94117. 415-931-1830. *Innkeepers:* Lisa and William Benau and Shirley and Paul Weber. Open all year.

This Queen Anne Victorian inn was built in 1897, Queen Victoria's Diamond Jubilee year. The house, given historic-landmark status by the city of San Francisco, stands across from the panhandle of Golden Gate Park. The inn's "belvedere," or open tower, topped by a teahouse roof and with a balustraded porch is one of only two left in the city.

The Victorian Inn, formerly known as the Clunie House, was designed by William Curlett, who also built other notable private and public buildings in San Francisco, including the pre-earthquake City Hall and the Crocker Mansion on Nobb Hill. The Clunie House stood through the elegance of the Victorian era, the San Francisco earthquake, world wars, the Depression, the "flower children" period, and more. Today, with a new lease on life, furnished with antiques from the turn of the century, the mansion invites visitors to relive the past in its high-ceilinged old rooms. Breakfast is served to guests; and later in the day, sherry is set out by the fireside in the Victorian parlor, and wine tastings are held in the evening. Fresh flowers, comforters, working fireplaces, and views of the park all enhance the rooms.

*Accommodations:* 12 rooms with private bath. *Pets and very young children:* Not permitted. *Driving Instructions:* Take the Fell Street exit off U.S. 101. The inn is at the corner of Fell and Lyon streets.

## WHITE SWAN INN

845 Bush Street, San Francisco, CA 94108. 415-775-1755. *Innkeeper:* Kelly O'Connell. Open all year.

White Swan Inn provides guests the ambience of a small English country-garden inn amid the dazzle and fun of cosmopolitan San Francisco. The five-story 1908 hotel, built just after the San Francisco earthquake, has been restored and redecorated with warm woods, soft rich colors, and English porcelains. The reception area sets the mood. The living room and a very British library invite guests to relax, and the dining room, where breakfast is served, overlooks a small courtyard and its English-style flower garden. The British tone is continued in the hotel's guest rooms, which have softly colored English wallpapers, comfortable sitting areas, fresh flowers, color-television sets, bedside telephones, and working fireplaces. Each has a private, tiled bathroom, complete with fluffy towels and scented soaps.

*Accommodations:* 26 rooms with private bath. *Pets:* Not permitted. *Driving instructions:* From Highway 101 (Van Ness Avenue with San Francisco), take Bush Street (one way). The inn is between Mason and Taylor.

## San Jose, California

### BRIAR ROSE BED & BREAKFAST INN

897 East Jackson Street, San Jose, CA 95112. 408-279-5999. *Innkeepers:* Cheryl and James Fuhring. Open all year.

Briar Rose Inn, which began as 1875 Victorian farmhouse in a walnut orchard, is now flanked by two neighborhood parks and surrounded by flower gardens, arbors, and a heart-shaped pond. Three rooms have marble fireplaces, and all have lavish Victorian wallcoverings and period pieces. Brocade, needlepoint, satin, and velvet upholstery cover settées and armchairs of carved hardwoods. Guest rooms are decorated with marble-top walnut bureaus, Victorian love seats, large carved beds, antique prints, and period lighting fixtures.

Tennis, bocci, and bicycle riding are available in the adjacent park; wineries, historic sites, and restaurants are nearby. Guests awaken to fresh-baked muffins and breads.

*Accommodations:* 5 rooms, 3 with private bath; 2 cottages. *Pets and smoking:* Not permitted. *Driving Instructions:* From the Freeway, take Route 101 northwest to 19th Street. Turn left and drive a short distance to Jackson Street; turn right to the inn.

## San Luis Obispo, California

### HERITAGE INN

978 Olive Street, San Luis Obispo, CA 93405. 805-544-7440. *Innkeepers:* Jim and Zella Harrison. Open all year.

At the turn of the century the house that is now the Heritage Inn stood at the junction of Route 1 and U.S. 101. It had been built by a family with many children, hence its many bedrooms. In 1930 the house was sold and moved to another street and then moved again to the present junction of Route 1 and U.S. 101, where it began a new life as an inn.

Today the inn is a bed-and-breakfast establishment with country antiques and six working fireplaces, four in guest rooms. The rooms without fireplaces have other special features of their own, perhaps a terrace or window seat overlooking the San Luis Creek. There are many thoughtful touches at the Heritage Inn, including complimentary bubble bath for use in the old-fashioned claw-footed tubs, bathrobes, and shampoos. In the evening, wines and hors d'oeuvres are set out in the parlor. A breakfast of home-baked goods, fruits, and beverages awaits guests in the dining room.

*Accommodations:* 9 rooms, 3 with private bath. *Pets and smoking:* Not permitted. *Children:* Under 10 not permitted. *Driving Instructions:* From Los Angeles take the Morro Bay exit off U.S. 101 to Olive Street. From San Francisco take the Santa Rosa Street exit off U.S. 101 to Olive Street.

## MADONNA INN

100 Madonna Road, San Luis Obispo, CA 93401. 805-543-3000.

*Innkeepers:* Alex and Phyllis Madonna. Open all year.

No guide to historic inns would be complete without the Madonna Inn. This fantasy world of whimsey and kitsch rolls Disneyland, Hansel and Gretel's gingerbread house, and the Flintstone's spread in Bedrock all into one. Madonna is the brainchild of Alex and Phyllis Madonna, who opened their first twelve rooms in 1958. Almost thirty years and 109 creations later, the inn attracts thousands of visitors annually to its colorful portals. This is one place guaranteed to make you smile. Like snowflakes, no two rooms are alike, and each gives new meaning to the word "unique."

In addition to the guest rooms, all of which can be perused in a picture book at the registration desk, there are clothing and gourmet shops and a bakery where rich delicacies are created for the Madonna's restaurants. The dining room and coffee shop serve three meals daily to guests and the public.

The Madonnas have chosen their favorite, albeit not terribly subtle, colors for use throughout the inn: Shocking pinks, golds, and reds. There are cupids, waterfalls, circular staircases, carved woods, and sparkling gold and crystal chandeliers everywhere.

The most special, and the hands-down favorites with guests, are the rock rooms. Some are virtual caves; one sleeps completely ensconsed in giant rock slabs like a Neanderthal's dream of heaven, complete with stone hearths, luxurious king-size beds, and fanciful bathrooms of rock with waterfalls cascading over towering monoliths. The rock rooms are usually booked far in advance, but there are other equally whimsical creations awaiting the adventurous.

*Accommodations:* 109 rooms with private bath. *Pets:* Not permitted. *Driving instructions:* The inn is just off Route 101, about midway between Los Angeles and San Francisco.

# THE BAYBERRY

111 West Valerio Street, Santa Barbara, CA 93101. 805-682-3199.
*Innkeeper:* Keith Pomeroy. Open all year.

This bed-and-breakfast inn began in 1896 as the summer residence for the French Ambassador and was later used for a variety of purposes before becoming an inn in 1981. There are five working fireplaces, four in guest rooms and one in the parlor, which is a favorite spot for guests to converse or read. Each of the guest rooms is named and decorated after a favorite berry. The Raspberry Room features hand-printed raspberry wallcovering imported from Paris. The Blueberry Room has a large bathroom with a claw-footed tub and a view over the treetops to the mountains. Breakfast is served on the sun deck, in the sun parlor or, on some occasions, in the mirrored dining room. Bicycles are available for leisurely expeditions, and the beach is just ten minutes away.

*Accommodations:* 8 rooms with private bath. *Smoking:* Not permitted. *Children:* Discouraged. *Driving Instructions:* From the north on 101, exit at Mission, turn left to De La Vina, right to Valerio, and left one block to the inn. From the south on 101, pass State Street by one block and turn right on Chapala, go north to Valerio, where you turn left and park.

## BLUE QUAIL INN

1908 Bath Street, Santa Barbara, CA 93101. 805-687-2300. *Innkeeper:* Jeanise Suding Eaton. Open all year except Christmas.

The Blue Quail Inn is a tidy California bungalow in a quiet residential section of Santa Barbara. The house and its accompanying small cottages were built in 1918, and in 1981 innkeeper Jeanise Suding opened it as a bed-and-breakfast inn. Guests have a choice of staying in one of the attractively decorated cottages set amid landscaped grounds or in either of two rooms in the main house. Each of the suites and rooms is named after a bird and appropriately decorated. The Oriole Suite, with its bright colors, has a large iron bed and old-fashioned wicker furnishings; the Nightingale Suite contains a fireplace in its living room and a canopied bed; the Cardinal Suite has a country theme; and the Meadowlark Room has a large bay window with a window seat. Guests are served a full breakfast in the dining room or on the patio. In the afternoon and evening, wine, juices and hone-baked snacks are served. Jeanise will pack picnic lunches on request, and she provides bicycles for guests' use in exploring the area.

*Accommodations:* 8 rooms, most with private bath. *Pets and smoking:* Not permitted. *Driving Instructions:* From U.S. 101 southbound take the Mission Street exit and turn left. Drive one block and turn right onto Castillo Street. Drive one block and turn left onto Pedregosa Street. Drive one block and turn left onto Bath Street.

## GLENBOROUGH INN AND COTTAGE

1327 Bath Street, Santa Barbara, CA 93101. 805-966-0589. *Inn-keepers:* David and Judy Groom and Laurel Ford. Open all year. The Glenborough Inn and its 1880 cottage nearby combine as a turn-of-the-century hostelry in the coastal town of Santa Barbara. The main house has a parlor complete with a wood-burning stove and fine old Victrola. Hors d'oeuvres, wine, and juices are served by the fireside in the evenings.

Upstairs in the main house are four guest rooms decorated with character and flair. The French Rose Room has a velvet rose spread on its antique French inlaid bed and wallpaper printed with tiny roses, as well as crocheted curtains that enhance the mountain views from three windows across one wall. The little Garden Room's brass-and-iron antique bed is covered with a white and green quilt. The rooms share two tiled baths with showers and deep tubs. The Victorian cottage across the street includes two suites with fireplaces and two additional guest rooms, each with its own bath and private entrance. The bedroom of the Grand Suite has a bed with crocheted canopy and coverlet. Guests have private use of the enclosed garden and hot tub; bicycles are available for touring the area. Pat and Jo Ann's gourmet breakfasts, delivered to guests' rooms or the garden, might include cheese blintzes, a ginger poached pear and date bread, or an egg casserole smothered with cheeses and topped with sour cream and avocado.

*Accommodations:* 9 rooms, 4 with private bath. *Pets:* Not permitted. *Smoking:* In cottage suites only. *Children:* Under 12 not permitted. *Driving Instructions:* Take U.S. 101 into Santa Barbara to Carrillo. Turn east on Carrillo to Bath Street. Turn north and drive three and a half blocks to the inn.

*We appreciate hearing about your experiences. If you have comments, suggestions, or recommendations about these or other inns and historic hotels, please use the reader report form at the back of this book, or write to us in care of our publishers: Burt Franklin and Co., Inc., P.O. Box 856, New York, N.Y. 10014 U.S.A.*

## SMOKING / CHILDREN

Regulations regarding *smoking* and *children* have changed so frequently in recent years that it is nearly impossible to keep up with these concerns. It seems that innkeepers are very undecided about these issues—changing their rules on a seemingly weekly basis. We *strongly* suggest that if you are an ardent smoker or non-smoker or if you are traveling with children or, conversely, the absence of children is important to you, be sure to confirm the rules that are currently applicable at the time you make your reservation—regardless of what an inn has indicated its policy is in this book. It might even be wise to double-check just before arriving!

## SIMPSON HOUSE INN

121 East Arrellaga, Santa Barbara, CA 93101. 805-963-7067. *Innkeepers:* Glyn and Linda Davies and Gillean Wilson. Open all year. The Victorian Simpson House was built in 1874, an era when Santa Barbara was accessible only by stagecoach or sailing ship. Since the house was built prior to the construction of the city's wharf, its wide horizontal and structural beams were unloaded from ships into the sea and floated ashore. Today, Simpson House has hedges, sandstone walls, shade trees, English gardens, and lawns and winding pathways.

The common room has rose-colored velvet upholstered Victorian chairs and a sofa in a setting that includes Oriental carpets and walls lined with bookcases. Two guest rooms open onto verandas overlooking gardens and church spires. The porch is the setting for evening get togethers, where hors d'oeuvres are served, and for breakfast. Bicycles are available for guests' use, and English croquet is often played on the lawn.

*Accommodations:* 6 rooms, 5 with private bath. *Pets, smoking, and children:* Not permitted. *Driving Instructions:* From Route 101, take the Santa Barbara Street exit, turn right, and drive 13 blocks. Then turn left onto Arrellaga.

## VILLA ROSA INN

15 Chapala Street, Santa Barbara, CA 93101. 805-966-0851. *Inn-keeper:* Beverly Kirkhart. Open all year.

Villa Rosa is a Spanish-style inn built in the 1930s just a few steps from the water's edge. It has been restored and decorated in a contemporary style softened by such Spanish-colonial touches as the rounded adobe-style archways, plantation shutters, and louvered doors. Rough-hewn beams, wooden and wrought-iron balconies, and Spanish tiles enhance the setting. The inn encloses a pool and spa, and the lounge is a favorite spot with guests, who enjoy the complimentary sherry, port, and cheeses served there in the evening. Each guest room is furnished with comfortable modern upholstered pieces in the cool purples, blues, and grays of the mountains, and four rooms have gas-burning tiled fireplaces. Fresh flowers, a long-stemmed rose, mints on the pillow at night, private baths and phones, and breakfast brought to the room are all part of the special service at the inn, which is within easy walking distance of the wharf shops and the harbor. The staff will gladly arrange dinner reservations.

*Accommodations:* 18 rooms with private bath. *Pets and children:* Not permitted. *Driving Instructions:* From the freeway (101) take the Chapala exit in Santa Barbara.

*Santa Clara, California*

## MADISON STREET INN

1390 Madison Street, Santa Clara, CA 95050. 408-249-5541. *Innkeepers:* Ralph and Theresa Wigginton. Open all year.

Madison Street Inn is a tidy 1891 Queen-Anne–style bed-and-breakfast inn with gingerbread detailing on the porch and eaves, set behind a white picket fence and shaded by pepper trees. The Wiggintons carried out a Victorian theme when they completed the decor, chosing authentic reproductions of lavish, turn-of-the-century screened paper. One guest room has a tall four-poster bed with a lace comforter, while others have brass beds, plush carpets, and Oriental rugs or contemporary furnishings that complement the Victorian antiques.

Hot breakfasts, which might include Belgian waffles or eggs Benedict, are served either in bed or in the dining room, which overlooks the swimming pool and hot tub, and, in the evening, sherry is served in the parlor. Theresa and Ralph provide bicycles for guests.

*Accommodations:* 5 rooms, 3 with private bath. *Pets and smoking:* Not permitted. *Children:* Family room available. *Driving instructions:* From Route 101, drive south to the San Tomas Expressway. Take San Tomas south to El Camino, turn left and continue 1 mile to Madison. Turn right; the inn is at the corner of Lewis and Madison.

*Santa Cruz, California*

## THE BABBLING BROOK INN

1025 Laurel Street, Santa Cruz, CA 95060. 408-427-2437. *Innkeepers:* Helen King. Open all year.

The Babbling Brook Inn is set into a steep Santa Cruz hillside in a bower of redwood and laurel trees, terraced gardens, stone walls, footbridges, waterfalls, and, of course, a babbling brook. The heart of this redwood inn is the original chinked log cabin built by several silent-movie actors in 1909. The inn has had a colorful history, with an equally colorful succession of owners, including the Russian Czar's last representative to the United States and a purported Austrian countess.

Today the inn is decorated along country-French lines with tiny-print wallpapers, lace curtains, pine and other antique furniture, and lots of fresh flowers. Ten of the guest rooms have wood-burning stoves, two have whirlpool baths, and several have their own private decks overlooking the brook and gardens. Off-street parking, telephones, and television sets are all provided. A country-style breakfast and afternoon wine are included.

*Accommodations:* 12 rooms with private bath. *Pets:* Not permitted. *Children:* Under 13 not permitted. *Driving Instructions:* In Santa Cruz take Route 1 north. At the fourth traffic light (Laurel Street) turn left towards the ocean and drive 2 blocks.

## CLIFF CREST BED & BREAKFAST INN

407 Cliff Street, Santa Cruz, CA 95060. 408-427-2609. *Innkeepers:* Sharon and Bruce Taylor. Open all year except Christmas.

Cliff Crest lives up to its name, perched as it is at the top of Beach Hill overlooking Monterey Bay. This historic landmark is a Queen Anne Victorian built in 1887. In the 1890s it was the home of William Jeter, a former lieutenant governor of California. With the assistance of his close friend John McLaren, landscape designer of San Francisco's Golden Gate Park, Jeter had the spacious grounds landscaped.

Two special features of the inn are its semicircular solarium and the second-story belvedere and balustrade looking out over the gardens. The Empire Room has a four-poster, king-size bed and fireplace. Upstairs, the Rose Room is the sunny master bedroom, with views of Monterey Bay and the Santa Cruz Mountains. Victorian furnishings and a claw-footed tub set the period tone of this room, whereas stained glass and a pineapple-carved four-poster bed are the highlights of the Pineapple Room. A full breakfast is served in the guests' rooms or in the solarium, and refreshments are offered in the evenings.

*Accommodations:* 5 rooms with private bath. *Pets, smoking, and children:* Not permitted. *Driving Instructions:* Take Route 17 to Ocean Street in Santa Cruz. Follow Ocean Street until it ends at San Lorenzo Boulevard. Turn right onto San Lorenzo, proceed to the traffic light, and turn left at Riverside Drive, cross the river, then proceed to Third Street and turn right. Take Third Street uphill to Cliff Street and turn left.

## DARLING HOUSE—BED & BREAKFAST BY THE SEA

314 West Cliff Drive, Santa Cruz, CA 95060. 408-458-1958. *Innkeepers:* Karen and Darrell Darling. Open all year.

A wealthy cattle baron commissioned an opulent Spanish Revival-style mansion in 1910 in an idyllic setting on a hillside overlooking the Pacific Ocean. No expense was spared. Darling House has intricately inlaid walls and floors, pressed copper flashings on the tiled roof, Venetian tile hearths, beveled-glass bookcases, and hundred of beveled-glass window panes. Museum-quality furnishings by Tiffany, Chippendale, and other early craftsmen compliment the rooms, most of which have views of the ocean. One guest room, with a working fireplace, has a telescope for observing whales and seals; another has light from Louis Tiffany's first patented electric lamp, which was created from a nautilus shell.

Breakfast includes warm breads baked with the inn's own organic walnuts and raisins. Guests may stroll through the citrus orchard or walk along a secluded beach. Coconut Grove Ballrom and seafood restaurants are a short walk.

*Accommodations:* 8 rooms, 2 with private bath; 1 cottage. *Pets:* Not permitted. *Smoking and children:* In cottage only. *Driving Instructions:* In Santa Cruz, take Route 1 (Mission Street) to Bay Street. Turn south and drive to West Cliff Drive. Turn right on Gharkey Street to the inn.

## MELITTA STATION INN

5850 Melita Road, Santa Rosa, CA 95409. 707-538-7712. *Innkeeper:* Diane Crandon and Vic Amstadter. Open all year.

Melitta Station Inn is in Sonoma Valley, the lush wine district known as the Valley of the Moon, just 5 miles east of Santa Rosa. It is in a late-nineteenth-century railroad station that later served as a freight depot where basalt stones quarried from the nearby hills were shipped by rail to San Francisco to be used for cobblestone streets. Today the redwood building is flanked by two state parks, the surrounding hills, pastures, and a little creek that flows behind it. Diane and Vic have created a country atmosphere with gardens, baskets and planters of colorful flowers, vines, and herbs. Inside, antique furnishings are nicely set off by the simplicity of the sunny rooms, oiled-fir floors have colorful throw rugs, and fresh white walls display hand stenciling. Scrolly iron beds have quilts, and antique bureaus have tiny bouquets of fresh flowers in season. The sitting room, which opens through French doors to a patio, has a wood-burning stove in one corner and a Welsh sideboard in another. Here wine is set out in the evening and, in the morning, breakfast, the only meal served, featuring egg and cheese dishes, baked apples, homemade scones, muffins, and fruit tortes. The parks across the road offer horseback riding and biking, and there is a small lake for sailing and rowing.

*Accommodations:* 6 rooms, 4 with private bath. *Pets and smoking:* Not permitted. *Children:* Inquire first. *Driving Instructions:* Follow the Sonoma Highway (Route 12) to Melita Road (just past the Calistoga Road). Turn right on Melita Road and go about a mile to Melitta Station Inn.

# Sausalito, California

## THE CASA MADRONA HOTEL AND RESTAURANT

801 Bridgeway, Sausalito, CA 94965. 415-332-0502. *Innkeeper:* John W. Mays. Open all year.

In 1885 a wealthy Vermont-born lumber baron named William G. Barrett bought a picturesque hillside property in Sausalito and proceeded to build his dream house high above the village. The Italianate home was a monument to the Victorian era, with marble fireplaces, stained-glass windows, brass chandeliers, and elaborate wrought-iron grillwork. Although Sausalito was ravaged by fire in 1893, the mansion escaped untouched except for some damage to the gardens. The manor house was a private home until 1910, when it was converted to a guest house. Throughout the first half of this century the Casa Madrona Hotel underwent a gradual decline. By the 1950s it had become a combination beer hall and boardinghouse serving the beat generation. It was salvaged from the brink of ruin by the Deschamps family, who installed antiques and accoutrements and gradually transformed the inn into a European-style pension. The heavy rains of 1973–74 threatened to close the inn, and only the intervention of John Mays saved it. Mays saw tremendous business potential in the property, bought it, and continued its restoration. In 1979 Mays became convinced that mud slides would always threaten the Casa Madrona. He and a group of architects and engineers began to design a project that would at once stabilize the lower hillside, preserve the historic Casa Madrona, and add additional guest accommodations that would provide twentieth-century amenities in an architectural setting complementary to the original building at the top of the hill. Construction began in 1981, and with two years sixteen suites had been completed, each decorated by a different Bay Area designer. The Salon Nouveau, for example, reflects the elegance of the Art Nouveau era with lush purple and mauve tones. The suite includes a canopied bed, wet bar, fireplace, and deck. The Madrona Villa, the largest suite, spans three terraced galleries and has brass appointments, botanical prints, a redwood-trimmed fireplace, and a rooftop deck with a view of the yacht-filled harbor.

Rooms in the historic portion of the Casa Madrona were decorated with carefully selected Victorian and other period antiques. The Regency Room includes a king-size canopied brass bed, a velvet love seat, and an antique English desk. White wicker furniture and shutters set the

tone of the Wicker Room, whereas an unusual mahogany fireplace is the focal point of the Fireside Room. The La Salle Room has a Jacuzzi with views of the bay. In addition to the historic and new sections of the hotel, there are five restored cottages.

The Casa Madrona Restaurant, on the hillside overlooking the harbor, offers candlelit dining, featuring American–California cuisine. Specialties include fresh local fish, roast quail, and medallions of veal.

*Accommodations:* 38 rooms with private bath, plus 5 cottages. *Pets:* Not permitted. *Driving Instructions:* From San Francisco, take U.S. 101 over the Golden Gate Bridge and use the first exit (Alexander Avenue) to downtown Sausalito. Casa Madrona is 100 yards past the first light.

## THE SAUSALITO HOTEL

16 El Portal, Sausalito, CA 94965. 415-332-4155. *Innkeeper:* Liz MacDonald. Open all year.

The Sausalito Hotel was built in 1900 in the ornate Mission Revival style so popular at the turn of the century. The two-story corner hotel has a series of second-floor bay windows that serve the guest rooms, plus a particularly striking corner round bay. The first floor of the hotel is devoted to shops; the guest rooms and small lobby occupy the second floor.

Rooms are furnished with Victorian antiques, decorated with appropriate wallpapers and swagged curtains at the windows, and have a hanging Victorian-style ceiling lamp. The Queen Victoria room has two armchairs set into the curved large bay mentioned above, as well as a carved high-back Victorian bed and matching marble-top dresser. In the Marquis de Queensberry room, you can recline in splendor on an elaborate bed, rivaling the one in the Vallejo Room at the Sonoma Hotel, that was once occupied by General Ulysses S. Grant. The room has the added attraction of a curved brick corner fireplace. Other guest rooms, while not on such a grand scale, offer comfort and elegance befitting the period.

The hotel is adjacent to the San Francisco ferry and surrounded by the many shops, restaurants, and galleries of this popular seaside village. At one time, bootleggers sought refuge in the Sausalito Hotel, and it is believed that Baby Face Nelson hid out here for a short while. Times are quieter now. The only meal served is the Continental breakfast, but there are many fine local restaurants, including Le Vivoir at the nearby Casa Madrona Inn.

*Accommodations:* 15 rooms, 10 with private bath. Parking is included in the room rates. *Driving Instructions:* Take the first exit (Alexander Avenue) off the Golden Gate Bridge north of San Francisco and follow to downtown Sausalito. The hotel is past the ferry on the right.

## THE SEAL BEACH INN AND GARDENS

212 Fifth Street, Seal Beach, CA 90740. 213-493-2416. *Innkeeper:* Marjorie Bettenhausen. Open all year.

Seal Beach Inn, only 300 yards from the ocean and with the look and feel of a French Mediterranean inn, is set in the hub of southern California, whose Disneyland, Knotts Berry Farm, and *Queen Mary* are all less than a half hour's drive away. Seal Beach, a picturesque coastal town with harbor and boutiques, is with a few blocks of the Long Beach marina. Innkeeper Marjorie Bettenhausen has created a *petite auberge,* complete with a flower-bedecked courtyard. Tubs of tropical trees and plants, a lacy iron fence imported from France, and antique streetlamps add their own special flavor to the inn.

A central library–drawing room has a fireplace, its oaken mantel trimmed with blue ornamental tiles. The inn's furnishings are a blend of family antiques and collectible art.

Guests spend their nights in rooms decorated with antiques. There are Cottage Studios and Royal Villas. Most rooms have sitting areas and kitchenettes. A complimentary full breakfast is served in the Tea Room or in the pool area.

*Accommodations:* 23 rooms with private bath. *Pets, smoking, and children:* Not permitted. *Driving Instructions:* Take the Seal Beach Boulevard exit from the Route 405 freeway. Take Seal Beach Boulevard to the Pacific Coast Highway and turn right. Drive a few blocks to Fifth Street, then turn left and drive 2 blocks to the inn.

## Sonoma, California

### OVERVIEW FARM

15650 Arnold Drive, Sonoma, CA 95476. 707-938-8574. *Innkeepers:* Judy and Robert Weiss. Open all year.

Overview Farm, on part of an original land grant from General Vallejo, is an 1800s hip-roofed Victorian, once part of the Spreckels estate. On five acres of oaks and madrones and overlooking the Sonoma Valley, the inn is furnished with a variety of antiques, ranging from Early American to Victorian. Spacious rooms have a fresh, airy look, with white walls, high ceilings, and many windows. Quilts cover antique bedsteads. Two guest rooms have working fireplaces, and on cool days a fire burns in the living room hearth. Breakfast is served in the dining room. A tree-shaded patio and gardens are available for guests' enjoyment.

*Accommodations:* 3 rooms with private bath.. *Pets and smoking:* Not permitted. *Children:* Not permitted. *Driving Instructions:* From Sonoma Plaza drive west to Arnold Drive; turn north and go approximately 4 miles. Turn west at the sign for the inn and drive to the end of the road.

## SONOMA HOTEL

110 West Spain Street, Sonoma, CA 95476. 707-996-2996. *Innkeepers:* John and Dorene Musilli. Open all year.

In 1835, the Mexican authorities were alarmed: Russian settlers had made inroads on the northern California coast, even going so far as to set up a fortress at Fort Ross, north of what is today Jenner. So Lieutenant Mariano Vallejo was dispatched to establish a military outpost in the area north of San Francisco and keep an eye on the Russians. A logical spot for such an outpost, it seemed to Vallejo, was at the beautiful Mission San Francisco de Solano, in the area now called Sonoma. Settling in quickly, he built adobe barracks for his soldiers, laid out a plaza, and built a home for himself and his family. Needing a name for his new pueblo, he chose "Sonoma," the Miwok Indian word for "valley of the moon."

Today you can sleep in the bed previously owned by Vallejo's sister. This carved-rosewood masterpiece rises to within inches of the wainscoted ceiling in Room 3, the Vallejo Room. The bed and its accompanying matched furniture are on loan from the Sonoma League of Historic Preservation. This bedroom and sixteen others, beautifully decorated with selections of matching and complementing antique furniture, constitute the historic Sonoma Hotel.

Built in the 1870s, the hotel has had a varied and colorful history. It has housed a bar, a mercantile hall, a meeting hall, a boarding house, and, for a time, the Plaza Hotel operated by the Sebastiani wine family. The present owners set about the monumental task of restoring it to a glory that certainly exceeds that of its predecessors. Do not despair if Room 3 is already booked. Rooms of almost equally exciting antiquity await your reservation. Take, for example, Room 1 with the most impressive brass bed we have laid eyes on; Room 4 with its armoire of inlaid parquet; Room 2 with a five-piece matching suite with hand-carved designs topped by rare orange marble; or Room 6 with its solid oak bedroom set inlaid with ebony and an antechamber ideal for reading. Third-floor rooms run to the smaller sizes and are somewhat lower in price but have many choice antiques. A Continental breakfast is served to overnight guests. The hotel's highly acclaimed restaurant and bar offer lunches and dinners to the public, using fresh seasonal ingredients prepared in imaginative ways. The antiques, fresh floral bouquets, and candlelight make the meals special.

*Accommodations:* 17 rooms, 5 with private bath. *Pets:* Not permitted. *Driving Instructions:* Sonoma is on Route 12 about 46 miles northeast of San Francisco.

## THISTLE DEW INN

171 West Spain Street, Sonoma, California. Mailing address: Box 1326, Sonoma, CA 95476. 707-938-2909. *Innkeepers:* Marv and Sunny Adams. Open all year.

The Thistle Dew Inn is actually two single-story turn-of-the-century Victorian homes on the same site. At the inn's entrance a low wall of locally quarried rock is covered with climbing plants, and a latticed garden between the front and rear houses is filled with tropical bromeliads, ferns, and hibiscus. Off the rear house is a latticed deck with hanging plants.

Both houses are furnished with Stickley pieces. The front house contains the main dining area — where a full breakfast is served — as well as a common sitting room with a free-standing soapstone fireplace. Wines and appetizers are served in the early evening on the deck. The house in back has another common sitting room and four guest rooms. One, the original master bedroom, has access to the deck. All the rooms have ceiling fans, queen-size beds, down pillows, fresh flowers, and central air-conditioning.

*Accommodations:* 6 rooms, 4 with private bath. *Pets and smoking:* Not permitted. *Children:* Under 12 not permitted. *Driving Instructions:* Take Route 12 to Sonoma. The inn is three houses from the northwest corner of the Plaza.

## *Sonora, California*

## THE RYAN HOUSE

153 South Shepherd Street, Sonora, CA 95370. 209-533-3445. *Innkeepers:* Nancy and Guy Hoffman. Open all year.

Ryan House is a small nineteenth-century home behind a picket fence, with old-fashioned flower gardens and a front walk lined with sweet-smelling roses. The Hoffmans have furnished it with antiques and Victorian reproductions. The guest rooms are decorated in soft, pastel shades selected to best display the quilts and antique furnishings in each room. Lavender Room has a handmade log-cabin quilt in hues of purple that is matched even by the room's pedestal sink. The parlor, with its wood-burning stove, is where guests often visit with the innkeepers over a glass of sherry. Afternoon tea and treats welcome arriving guests. Breakfasts are served in the dining room. Ryan House, although in a quiet neighborhood, is just two blocks from downtown, where there are restaurants, shops, and historic sites.

*Accommodations:* 4 rooms, 2 with private bath. *Pets and smoking:* Not permitted. *Driving instructions:* From Route 108, drive north one block on Route 49; turn east and go two blocks to the corner of Shepherd.

## Sutter Creek, California

### NINE EUREKA STREET

55 Eureka Street, Sutter Creek, California. Mailing address: P.O.
Box 386, Sutter Creek, CA 95685. 209-267-0342. *Innkeeper:* Nancy and Bob Brahmst. Open February through November.

Sutter Creek, a small Gold Country village, is home to Nine Eureka
Street, a classic California Bungalow that has traditional clean lines,
a rich patina of time-softened woodwork, and many stained-glass windows. Its rooms are filled with turn-of-the-century antiques. Some
rooms offer views of the surrounding hills. The sitting room frequently
has a lively game of cards in progress, or one might find guests comparing the day's adventures. Nancy serves a family-style breakfast to
guests in the dining room.

In addition to the multitude of Gold-Country historical attractions
nearby, there are lakes, golf courses, and ski areas, all within a thirty-
minute drive of the inn. The rural roads nearby are also ideal for hiking
and bicycling.

*Accommodations:* 5 rooms with private bath. *Pets and smoking:*
Not permitted. *Children:* Discouraged. *Driving instructions:* The inn
is two blocks off Route 49.

## SUTTER CREEK INN

75 Main Street, Sutter Creek, California. Mailing Address: Box 385, Sutter Creek, CA 95685. 209-267-5606 (keep ringing). *Innkeeper:* Jane Way. Open all year.

Settled comfortably in the middle of this lovely gold-country town is the Sutter Creek Inn. As former New Englanders, it is easy for us to see what tugged at Jane Way's heartstrings when she first saw the handsome Greek Revival building with its distinct New England lines. One must presume that the look was chosen to placate the owner's bride, who had been transplanted from her native New Hampshire. When Jane first saw the place, in the mid-1960s, it was empty and looked a bit forlorn. It is hardly that now. It is crisply painted with its clapboard gleaming and its doors and shutters in pleasant contrasting tones. Inside, the main house has a large living room and a breakfast room with two big harvest tables for Jane's daily morning repast, the only meal served, but a full American-style meal it is.

Rooms vary in size. Some are in the main inn; others, behind in the former outbuildings, recently converted to overnight accommodations. The choice of rooms is considerable, and prices vary accordingly. Some have beds that hang suspended from the ceilings by chains but can be stabilized. These beds have become Jane's trademark and are sought after by many of her guests. Ten rooms have fireplaces with a supply of firewood provided. The names of the rooms are, in some cases, more prosaic than their attractive decorations. Thus you may stay in Tool Shed, Miner's Cabin, or Lower Washhouse. Definitely not prosaic is the Carriage House with a fireplace, queen-size bed, and two bathrooms. It is the inn's most expensive room.

The living room of the 1859 house is filled with the latest books and magazines, a piano, and game tables. The roomy kitchen has a big fireplace where guests sip coffee and tea until the breakfast gong summons them to a family-style start of the day. Handwriting analysis is offered each morning in the living room. Appointments can be made upon guests' arrival.

*Accommodations:* 19 rooms with private bath. *Pets:* Not permitted. *Children:* Under 15 not permitted. *Driving Instructions:* The inn is 4 miles north of Jackson on Route 49.

## Tahoe City, California

### MAYFIELD HOUSE

236 Grove Street, Tahoe City, California. Mailing address: P.O. Box 5999, Tahoe City, CA 95730. Reservations: 916-583-1001. *Innkeepers:* Bruce and Cynthia Knauss. Open all year.

Mayfield House, built in 1932, is a steeply gabled private home that was converted into a bed-and-breakfast inn in the North Lake Tahoe country. Guest rooms have been distinctively decorated and named: Upstairs is the Mayfield Room, the master bedroom, with a king-size bed, sitting area, and view of the mountains. Julia's Room, named after a frequent guest, Julia Morgan, contains a king-size bed and is decorated in soft blue shades. The Guest Room is on the landing, and three rooms on the first floor include The Den, The Study, and Mrs. Hinkle's Room. Each room offers down comforters, fresh flowers, brass and copper accents, and original watercolors by Margaret Carpenter.

Breakfast offers fresh juice, fruits, cheese, home-baked breads and pastries, preserves, and coffee or tea. Guests may be served in their rooms, on the terrace, in the breakfast room, or in the living room.

*Accommodations:* 6 rooms with 3 shared baths. *Pets and smoking:* Not permitted. *Children:* Under 12 not permitted. *Driving Instructions:* The inn is on Grove Street, off Route 28 (turn at the big pine tree in the middle of the highway).

## Templeton, California

### COUNTRY HOUSE INN

91 Main Street, Templeton, CA 93465. 805-434-1598. *Innkeeper:* Dianne Garth. Open all year.

Both the Country House and the peaceful village of Templeton date from 1886. The inn was the private estate of the town's developer, who arrived at the time Templeton was chosen to be the southern terminus of the Southern Pacific Railroad. Today the inn, a San Luis Obispo County historical landmark, retains the elegant hallmarks of those boomtown days — the 11-foot ceilings with gold-leaf moldings and the crystal chandeliers.

Guest rooms' names hint at each one's special flavor. Garden View, originally the parlor, has a king-size bed and a window seat. Summer Kitchen is decorated with country antiques, and Vintage Rose, in warm burgundies and roses, has a brass bed. Breakfast is served in the formal dining room.

*Accommodations:* 6 rooms, 3 with private bath. *Pets and smoking:* Not permitted. *Driving Instructions:* The inn is just off Route 101, about 20 miles north of San Luis Obispo.

*Venice, California*

## THE VENICE BEACH HOUSE

No. 15 Thirtieth Avenue, Venice, CA 90291. 213-823-1966. *Innkeeper:* Alfonso Perez-Pardo. Open all year.

The Venice Beach House is a landmark shingled California Craftsman–style bungalow built in 1911 for a family with eight daughters. The inn is surrounded by lawns and gardens with palms and ferns. Guests enter a 50-foot-long parlor from the trellised veranda. A bay window is the setting for a Continental breakfast and late-afternoon wine and cheese. The parlor, with its antique Persian rug, rose-colored velvet furnishings, and brick hearth, is filled with memorabilia including old photos and art of historic Venice Beach, as are the halls and the guest rooms, each of which was named for a character or event from the area's history. There are ocean views, several fireplaces, a balcony, canopied and brass beds, antiques, and quilts. The inn is 50 feet from a wide sandy beach and with easy reach of Hollywood, Beverly Hills, and Disneyland.

*Accommodations:* 9 rooms, 5 with private bath. *Pets and smoking:* Not permitted. *Driving Instructions:* Take the Marina Freeway (Route 90) exit off the San Diego Freeway (Route 405) and proceed west to Lincoln. Turn right on Lincoln, continue to Washington and turn left; drive toward the ocean. Turn right on Speedway. Drive past 30th Avenue (which is for pedestrians only) and turn right onto 29th Place, where guests may park.

## LA MER EUROPEAN BED AND BREAKFAST

411 Poli Street, Ventura, CA 93001. 805-643-3600. *Innkeeper:* Gisela Baida. Open all year.

La Mer European Bed and Breakfast is an 1890 New-England–style house that would be more likely spotted on Cape Cod. Gisela, a native of Siegerland, Germany, has transformed the inn into a European hostelry decorated with antiques of several countries. Guest rooms have a balcony or porch, a private entrance, and some, a sea view. Madame Pompadour is wonderfully Parisian, with wood-burning stove. Captains Coje has a Norwegian nautical theme and a large ship's bed. One sunny spot was transformed into a Bavarian-style breakfast room, where a buffet offers such treats as apple strudel, Blackforest ham, cheeses, and breads and croissants. Guests are given a complimentary bottle of wine or champagne as a special welcoming touch. The beach is with walking distance, and La Mer provides picnic baskets for hiking and sightseeing trips.

*Accommodations:* 5 rooms with private bath. *Pets and smoking:* Not permitted. *Children:* Under 13 not permitted. *Driving Instructions:* From Route 101 South, take the Main Street exit, turn left on Oak Street and proceed to Poli Street. From Route 101 North, take the California Street exit, follow to Poli Street and turn left.

## SAINT GEORGE HOTEL

16104 Volcano–Pine Grove Road, Volcano, California. Mailing address: P.O. Box 9, Volcano, CA 95689. 209-296-4458. *Innkeepers:* Marlene and Charles Inman. Open mid-February to January; closed Monday and Tuesday.

The Saint George Hotel is a modest three-story structure that managed to survive the rise and fall of this relatively well-preserved mining town. Two other hotels had flourished briefly on this same spot in the mid-nineteenth century, but the Eureka and the Imperial both succumbed to the most common disaster of the era — uncontrolled fire. The Saint George was constructed by its founder, B. F. George. Today, bedrooms are available on the two upper floors of the vine-covered, balconied building.

The rooms are furnished mostly with antiques. There is a lounge with a fireplace and an Old West bar with artifacts and pictures from the mining days. Rooms in the main hotel maintain the custom of the Gold Rush days of sharing a bath at the end of the hall on each floor. Hotel beds all have hand-crocheted bedspreads. A modern annex built in 1961 contains rooms with private bath.

Dinners feature a single entrée, frequently prime ribs of beef or chicken. Soups, breads, and desserts accompanying the meal are all made in the hotel kitchen. This is a quiet, unpretentious place in a town that has been largely untouched by the march of time. One can sit on the porch at twilight on an old bench, much as the miners did years ago, and hear the cry of a coyote from behind the limestone ruins of the old Wells Fargo office. It's not fancy, but it surely is peaceful.

*Accommodations:* 20 rooms, 6 with private bath (1 1/2 baths per floor). *Pets and children:* Permitted in annex rooms only. *Driving Instructions:* Drive east on Route 88 to Pine Grove, then north on Volcano–Pine Grove Road to Volcano.

## DEHAVEN VALLEY FARM

39247 North Highway 1, Westport, CA 95488. 707-964-5252. *Innkeeper:* Jim and Kathy Tobin. Open all year.

Dehaven Valley Farm has a resident ghost: A lonely young man who walks the upper halls when the tides are high and the surf pounds the rocky coast nearby. He disturbs no one and leaves the halls peacefully empty the rest of the year. The focus of this coastal inn is a Victorian farmhouse amid twenty acres of rolling meadows and forests that drop to the ocean just north of Mendocino. This setting is home to several barnyard creatures, including horses, donkeys, sheep, geese, rabbits, chickens, and cats.

The inn and several outbuildings provide antique-furnished guest rooms, some with fireplaces and sitting rooms, some tucked under the eaves and dormers. No matter where they are, guests can expect attractive wallpapers and thick, warm comforters on the beds.

The inn's large living room is a favorite gathering spot for guests, drawn to the crackling fire, the collection of good books, and the library of video-cassette-recorder tapes. The dining room provides fresh seasonal dishes prepared from produce grown on local farms and seafood from nearby fishing villages. The small but creative menu is enhanced by a good selection of wines.

In addition to the horses, bicycles are available, and a hot tub awaits guests' return. Picnics are provided on request.

*Accommodations:* 8 rooms, 6 with private bath. *Pets and smoking:* Not permitted. *Driving instructions:* The inn is 1.7 miles north of Westport, on Route 1.

# HOWARD CREEK RANCH

P.O. Box 121, Westport, CA 95488. 707-964-6725. *Innkeepers:* Charles (Sunny) and Sally Grigg. Open all year.

In 1867, Alfred Howard and his father arrived in this secluded valley and built themselves a ranch on a clear creek that rushes down from the surrounding mountains, bordered by grassy slopes that fall abruptly to the sea. The historic redwood house is little changed since those pioneer times. The redwood tongue and groove walls, the country antiques and family heirlooms, create an atmosphere that Sally likes to call "elegant-rustic." This early-California theme is enhanced by quilt-covered beds, hand-embroidered pillowcases, hanging plants, and hearty ranch breakfasts.

Flowers and wildlife abound in this spectacular topographic setting. A 75-foot hanging bridge over the creek leads to the ranch's old barn, the largest for many miles. The pool sits on the side of the mountain, as do a hot-tub and sauna. In the end, though, it is the Pacific that dominates—ever changing, ever present, ever beautiful. At low tide one can walk a 3-mile stretch of the beach without being noticed by anything but the birds and other shore life.

*Accommodations:* 7 rooms, including some in cabins, with bath. *Pets and children:* By prior arrangement. *Smoking:* Restricted. *Driving Instructions:* The ranch is 3 miles north of Westport. Call for directions.

## *Yosemite, California*

### AHWAHNEE HOTEL

Yosemite National Park, CA 95389. 209-252-4848. *Innkeeper:* Curt S. Abramson. Open all year.

During the mid-1920s the then director of the National Park Service, Stephen T. Mather, was embarrassed when a member of the English nobility refused to stay at the old Sentinel Hotel on the park grounds. Mather ordered the two rival concession companies on the grounds to stop bickering with each other and join forces to construct a luxury hotel. The Ahwahnee, the product of that rapprochement, in the final reckoning cost $1 million to build plus $250,000 for interior decoration. A serious effort was made to soundproof the building so that the roar of Yosemite Falls would not disturb light sleepers. Ultimately, defeat was admitted. Today, as in 1927, the sound of Yosemite's greatest falls lulls guests to sleep.

The building's grandeur is evident as soon as you enter the lobby.

Tall picture windows overlook the scenes of Yosemite Valley. The main dining room has huge sugar-pine beams and exposed granite columns rising to a ceiling height of 34 feet. During winter months, the Great Lounge fireplace sheds a glow in the evening. Tea is served there in the afternoon, and a demitasse at night.

The guest rooms are decorated with deep-colored floral fabrics and dark wood furnishings; colorful tiles are arranged in an Indian-type pattern in their private bathrooms. The spacious grounds include two tennis courts and a heated swimming pool. In addition to the rooms in the main building, there are several cottages by the hotel.

As at the Hotel Wawona, guests are expected to dress for dinner. The Continental menu offers such northwestern fish as salmon trout as well as beef, lamb, and chicken dishes. Chef's and Vintner's holidays, running from mid-November through January, offer seminars, wine tastings, and sessions with visiting chefs.

*Accommodations:* 123 rooms with private bath. *Pets:* Not permitted. *Driving Instructions:* Take Route 120, 140, or 41 to Yosemite National Park; follow the signs to Yosemite Valley. At Yosemite Village, follow the signs to the Ahwahnee Hotel.

## HOTEL WAWONA

Yosemite National Park, CA 95389. 209-375-6556. *Innkeeper:* Judy Durr. Open Easter through Thanksgiving.

This fine Victorian resort hotel got its start in 1856, when Galen Clark homesteaded in the Wawona basin. Mr. Clark was suffering from tuberculosis and had been told he had just a year or two left to live. He came to the mountains to die among the scenic wonders of Yosemite and proceeded to live for fifty-three more years, succumbing at the age of ninety-six.

The plot of land Clark chose to develop when he came to Yosemite was a full day's ride from the end of the stagecoach line. Thus he found himself playing host to many people forced to spend the night, and he was eventually prompted to build rooms to accommodate guests on a paying basis. In 1934, the land and hotel were sold to the National Park Service. Since then the hotel has been run by the current owners, Yosemite Park and the Curry Company, and is listed in the National Register of Historic Places.

This Victorian-era hotel has a white exterior and wide verandas that reflect the California heritage of Spanish haciendas. Hop vines decorate its front in the summer months. Towering incense cedar trees shade the lawn, and lawn chairs are scattered about much as they might have been fifty years ago.

The hotel's interior is furnished with antiques and decorated to conform to the atmosphere that prevailed in the late nineteenth century. The Sun Room in the Annex is a public lounge decorated with rattan furniture and inlaid wood paneling. Approximately half the guest rooms have antique bedsteads, either wood or brass. Each room opens onto the veranda overlooking the broad lawns surrounding the buildings. All guest rooms were completely redone in 1982.

The dinner menu at Wawona offers a wide selection of dishes, including grilled rainbow trout, Southern fried chicken, prime ribs of beef, and seafood.

*Accommodations:* 77 rooms, 48 with private bath. *Pets:* Not permitted. *Driving Instructions:* From Fresno, take Route 41 to Yosemite National Park; the hotel is set back from the road 6 miles inside the park. From other directions, after arriving in Yosemite take Wawona Road to the hotel.

*Yountville, California*

## BURGUNDY HOUSE COUNTRY INN

6711 Washington Street, Yountville, CA 94599. 707-944-0889. *Innkeepers:* Dieter and Ruth Back. Open all year.

In the heart of the wine country of Napa Valley, Burgundy House was built in the 1870s, by Charles Rouvegneau and his workers, as a distillery that would stand the test of time. They wrested native fieldstone from the surrounding countryside and put up 22-inch-thick walls around stout hand-hewn posts and beams. The result is a rough-stone, two-and-a-half-story historic structure that is cool in the summer and cozy around the huge hearth when days turn crisp.

Guest rooms are furnished in a country style, with pine and light oak antiques, fresh flowers, a decanter of local wine, and colorful quilts. Breakfast, which might include a special casserole or egg dish along with fruits, pastries, and cereals, is served in the "distillery" or in the garden.

*Accommodations:* 5 rooms with private bath. *Pets, smoking, and children:* Not permitted. *Driving Instructions:* Take 1-80 north from San Francisco to Route 29, and Route 29 north to Yountville and exit to Washington Street. Turn left.

## MAGNOLIA HOTEL

6529 Yount Street, Yountville, California. Mailing address: P.O. Drawer M, Yountville, CA 94599. 707-944-2056. *Innkeepers:* Bruce and Bonnie Locken. Open all year.

This hotel was built in 1873 of stones hauled from a nearby quarry. The adjoining building was constructed in 1900 of bricks rescued from an old church and had served previously as ballast for a ship that bore them from Europe. The stone walls are up to 28 inches thick. In days gone by, the hotel served as a bordello, a working man's hotel, a 4-H headquarters, and the local center for rum-running during Prohibition.

Today rooms have either exposed-brick or stone walls. Bedrooms have brass or carved Victorian headboards and antique furnishings, complimented by a decanter of port.

Adjacent to the hotel is the Garden Court, housing four guest rooms with king-size beds, bay windows, tiled baths, and fireplaces. A renovated carriage house, with two guest rooms, includes high tin ceilings, a gas-log fireplace, and bay windows overlooking gardens and vineyards. The rear of the hotel contains the heated Jacuzzi 12-foot spa that is used all year. A heated pool is also on the grounds.

Full breakfasts are served to houseguests in the dining room, connected to the inn via its rough-stone wine cellar. Hotel guests enter through a street-level entrance. Once inside they are surrounded the warm with the glow of the fireplace.

*Accommodations:* 12 rooms with private bath. *Pets and smoking:* Not permitted. *Driving Instructions:* Yountville is 9 miles north of Napa. Take the "Yountville-Veterans Home" exit off Route 29.

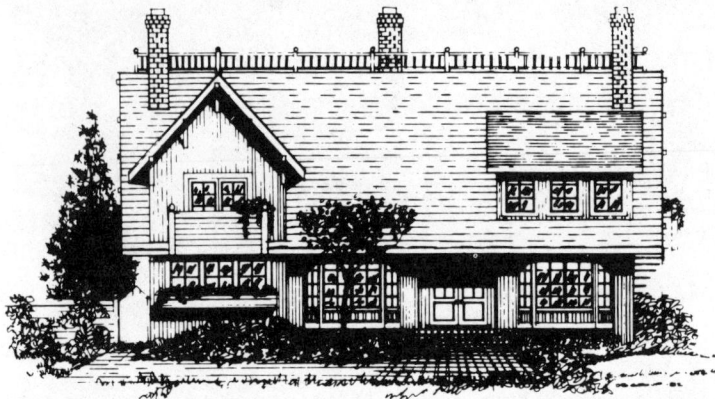

## OLEANDER HOUSE

7433 Saint Helena Highway, Yountville, California. Yountville, CA 94599. 707-944-8315. *Innkeeper:* John and Louise Packard. Open all year.

Oleander House, centrally located in wine country between the Domaine Chandon and Robert Mondavi wineries, was built in the early 1980s. Each guest room has a fireplace and deck and is decorated with Laura Ashley print wallpaper and coordinated bed coverings and dust ruffles. The rooms are furnished with country-French antiques and brass or iron beds, and all are air-conditioned. Guests are served a full breakfast from a different menu each day; complimentary brandy or soft drinks are available. Oleander House is just a short distance from the many wineries and restaurants of this area.

*Accommodations:* 4 rooms with private bath. *Pets, smoking, and children:* Not permitted. *Driving Instructions:* Oleander House is between Yountville and Oakville on the Saint Helena Highway (Route 29).

# Oregon

## Ashland, Oregon

## CHANTICLEER BED AND BREAKFAST INN

120 Gresham Street, Ashland, OR 97520. 503-482-1919. *Innkeepers:* Jim and Nancy Beaver. Open all year.

The Craftsman period of American architecture was characterized by rebellion against the ornamentation of the Victorian period that preceded it. Sometimes called the California Bungalow style, this form depended heavily on native materials and stressed open, flowing rooms with built-in furniture—all evident at the Chanticleer Inn.

Native river stones were used to construct the inn's porch, as well as the living room fireplace. The adjacent dining room has a view of the Cascade Mountain foothills and Bear Creek Valley. Breakfast is served here and features such specialties as "Dutch babies," German pancakes, custards with fresh fruit, and blintzes.

The inn has seven guest rooms: one on the main floor, two fashioned from former attic space, and four below in rooms that open out onto the hillside behind the inn. The lower-floor rooms have separate entrances from a brick patio. The popular Fleur, named for its floral prints, is among the nooks and crannies of the gabled roof. The inn is just four blocks from Ashland's Shakespeare Festival. Dinner–ski packages are available.

*Accommodations:* 7 rooms with private bath. *Pets, smoking, and children:* Not permitted. *Driving Instructions:* Turn west off Route 99 (Main Street) onto Gresham.

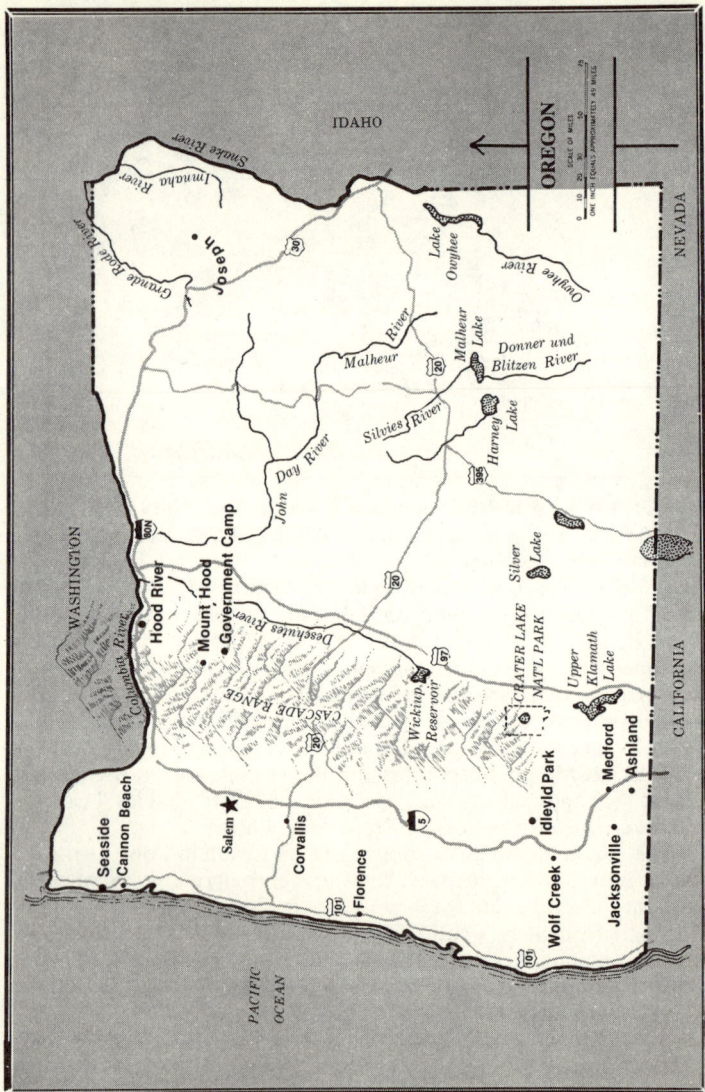

## EDINBURGH LODGE

586 East Main Street, Ashland, OR 97520. 503-488-1050. *Innkeeper:* Ann Rivera. Open all year.

Innkeeper Ann Rivera has brought her affection for Britain and English gardens to her English-style bed-and-breakfast inn. The house was built in 1908 as a boardinghouse for railroad workers and schoolteachers. It was restored and furnished with the early 1900s in mind, using old-fashioned wallpapers throughout and Victorian beds covered with lovely old quilts. Each guest room is named for a Scottish castle, and all have air-conditioning and queen-size or twin beds.

Breakfast may include such favorites as peaches-and-cream French toast, garden-vegetable eggs, or custard cornbread. Afternoon tea is served to those back from the day's activities.

*Accommodations:* 6 rooms with private bath. *Pets and smoking:* Not permitted. *Driving Instructions:* From I-5 take the Ashland exit to East Main Street near downtown Ashland.

## HERSEY HOUSE

451 North Main Street, Ashland, OR 97520. 503-482-4563. *Innkeepers:* Gail E. Orell and K. Lynn Savage. Open May through October.

Hersey House is a turn-of-the-century Victorian that was home to five generations of Herseys. The bed-and-breakfast inn is furnished with family heirlooms brought by sisters Gail and Lynn from their former home in Coos Bay. Guest rooms have air-conditioning, private baths, and queen-size beds. Eastlake Room has views of Mt. Ashland, and Wildflower Room has country-style pine antiques.

Breakfast is a festive affair served on family china, silver, and linens. Specialities might include ginger-bread pancakes with lemon curd or secret Eggs Hersey, accompanied by fresh-squeezed orange juice and pots of coffee and tea. An English-style garden supplies fresh bouquets and fruit in season. The inn is with a short walk of Ashland's plaza, theaters, and Lithia Park.

*Accommodations:* 4 rooms with private bath. *Pets and smoking:* Not permitted. *Children:* Under 12 not permitted. *Driving Instructions:* The inn is located at the northwest corner of Main and Nursery.

## IRIS INN

59 Manzanita Street, Ashland, OR 97520. 503-488-2286. *Innkeepers:* Vicki Lamb. Open all year.

A stained-glass window depicting three irises is the focal point of the entry hall at the Iris Inn. The window, set into the front door, introduces a floral theme that is carried on throughout the inn. Leaded windows light the landings of the stairway leading to the antique-furnished guest rooms, which offer views either of Bear Creek Valley and Grizzly Mountain or of Mount Ashland. The Rose Room has an old-fashioned iron bed covered with a quilt with a rose print fabric. The Jade Room has a floral-print quilt covering a painted iron bedstead, and iris prints enliven its deep green walls.

The inn was built in 1905 by Ashland pioneers, Mr. and Mrs. James Thornton, and was a residence until 1982, when Vicki and John Lamb turned it into a guest house. The sitting room is furnished with comfortable family pieces and is favorite spot for plotting the day's activities. The dining room is the setting for breakfast, which includes crepes, apple pancakes and buttermilk scones. There is a rose garden with a deck out back.

*Accommodations:* 5 rooms, 1 with private bath; 2 shared baths. *Pets and smoking:* Not permitted. *Driving Instructions:* From I-5 take exit 19. Turn left at the stoplight onto old U.S. 99, proceed 1.6 miles, and turn right onto Manzanita Street.

## MORICAL HOUSE

668 North Main Street, Ashland, OR 97520. 503-482-2254. *Innkeepers:* Pat and Peter Dahl. Open all year.

Morical House, on an acre of lawns, appears to be a late-nineteenth-century farmhouse with its many gables, each finished with a different style of shingle and trim, the result of several periods of construction that started in 1880. Intricate woodwork and stained-glass windows highlight the interior, whose public rooms include a spacious foyer with a fireplace, an adjacent parlor with an Eastlake-style carved pump organ, and well-stocked library shelves. The large dining room, where breakfast is served, has an attached porch with sweeping views of the Cascade Mountains. Throughout the inn, Oriental carpets add warmth to the wood floors, and guest rooms have handmade comforters, lace curtains with balloon valences, and wallpapers re-creating the late Victorian period. A third-floor guest room created from two

former attic bedrooms, and especially popular with honeymooners, has a large brass bed and painted "cottage" furniture. The inn's land-scaped grounds include a large outcropping of granite boulders, and hundreds of trees, shrubs, and flower beds surround the lawn and a special bent-grass putting green. Pat's generous breakfast includes breads, pastries or muffins, and such specialties as eggs Florentine, Belgian waffles, and omelets.

*Accommodations:* 5 rooms with private bath. *Pets and smoking:* Not permitted. *Children:* Under 12 not permitted. *Driving Instructions:* The inn is on Ashland's Main Street, just north of downtown.

# THE WINCHESTER INN

35 South Second Street, Ashland, OR 97520. 503-488-1113 or 488-1115. *Innkeepers:* Michael and Laurie Gibbs. Open all year. The Winchester Inn is about half a block from its original location, a half-block that rises practically straight up a hillside surrounded by tiered gardens and patios. The Queen Anne–style Victorian served as southern Oregon's first hospital in the early 1900s. Situated in downtown Ashland's historic district, the inn offers antique-filled guest rooms. One of these, the Garden Room, has a bay window overlooking the gardens, an antique iron bedstead, and wicker furnishings. The Queen Anne Suite has soft rose and plum decor and a matching set of antique Victorian furnishings. Some rooms have private patios or balconies with flower-filled window boxes in season.

The restaurant overlooks the gardens, which are lit at night. Breakfast is served in the period dining room to overnight guests, and dinners for the public feature fresh local seafood and a number of interesting ethnic dishes. The inn's decor, gardens, and gazebo make it popular for weddings and receptions.

*Accommodations:* 7 rooms with private bath. *Pets:* Not permitted. *Driving Instructions:* From I-5, take the Route 66 (Main Street) exit into downtown Ashland.

## HEARTHSTONE INN

Jackson and Hemlock, Cannon Beach, Oregon. Mailing address: P.O. Box 66, Tolovana Park, OR 97145. 503-436-2266. *Innkeepers:* Lisa and Richard Howell. Open all year.

Hearthstone Inn is located in an area of natural beauty near Cannon Beach, which is just six blocks from the inn and less than two hours from Portland. There are seven miles of beaches dotted with towering rocks, or monoliths, carved over the centuries by the sea. Haystack, at a height of 235 feet, is one of the world's largest. The area is a wildlife refuge, with many tidal pools on the beaches.

The inn, built in 1982, is surrounded by flower gardens that bloom all year. Cedar is used in the vaulted ceilings and most of the door and window trim as well as in many of the contemporary furnishings. Earth tones on the walls complement the natural woods, softly lit by skylights. Old-fashioned paddle fans cool rooms in the summer, and each room has its own beachstone fireplace. No meals are served, but there are several fine restaurants in the area.

Ecola State Park, two miles north of the inn, has hiking trails and secluded beaches, and it borders Wayside Park, the southernmost point of the Lewis and Clark Trail. Cannon Beach is home to many artists, with shops and galleries displaying and selling local works ranging from hand-blown glass and sculpture to fabric design. Theatrical productions are presented by a local summer-stock company.

*Accommodations:* 4 rooms with private bath. *Pets:* Not permitted. *Driving Instructions:* From Portland, take Route 26 west to Route 101 and drive south to Cannon Beach. The inn is 6 blocks south of town on the east side of Hemlock.

## MADISON INN

660 S. W. Madison Avenue, Corvallis, OR 97333. 503-757-1274. *Innkeepers:* Richard and Paige Down. Open all year.

Madison Inn is a 1903 Queen Anne–style house built with especially large rooms to accommodate the patients of the doctor who lived and worked here. Later, the large wood-framed building served as a fraternity house for nearby Oregon State University. It is now listed in the National Register of Historic Places.

Kathryn Brandis, mother of innkeeper Paige Down, raised her family here, and all of her children had a hand in the inn's restoration. Each room, furnished with antiques and family mementos, is named for a person who grew up in that room. The bay windows in the Paige and the Honore rooms look across the street to the rose gardens, gazebo, and fountains of Central Park. Oriental carpets in the common rooms set off the antique furnishings, and the rays of the afternoon sun are scattered by the prisms of leaded-glass windows. Collections of books are found everywhere. After a breakfast that includes special baked dishes, guests may wish to visit the Corvallis Art Center or the university campus or enjoy the numerous bicycling and walking paths throughout the city.

*Accommodations:* 7 rooms, 1 with private bath. *Pets:* Not permitted. *Smoking:* Restricted. *Driving Instructions:* Take I-5 to Route 34 and drive west toward Corvallis (about 10 miles). After crossing Willamette River Bridge, Route 34 becomes Harrison Boulevard. Continue to 5th Street, turn left, and then turn right on Madison.

## THE JOHNSON HOUSE

216 Maple Street, Florence, Oregon. Mailing address: P.O. Box 1892, Florence, OR 97439. 503-997-8000. *Innkeepers:* Jayne and Ron Fraese. Open all year.

Before taking up innkeeping, Jayne and Ron Fraese owned a print gallery in southern California. They have continued to collect antique prints and photographs, for which their inn is a perfect showcase. They have carefully restored the 1892 house, the town's oldest, to its original simplicity, a tribute to the early settlers of this scenic Oregon coastal community. Comfortable turn-of-the-century antiques are complemented by prints and photographs on the walls.

Bookshelves and cupboards are filled with books, periodicals from around the country, and an extensive collection of rare cartoon anthologies, essays, and short stories. Plenty of comfortable easy chairs and good reading lights are found throughout the inn. The guest rooms' antique furnishings include period beds with luxurious down comforters. The snug parlor is a fine spot for visiting with other guests over coffee or a glass of wine or beer. Breakfasts often include special soufflés, freshly baked fruit breads, muffins, and pots of tea and coffee. Local berry jams accompany the main dishes.

Johnson House is a block from the Siuslaw River, which runs to the sea nearby. The coast offers such recreational pleasures as crabbing, clamming, and mushrooming.

*Accommodations:* 5 rooms, 1 with private bath. *Pets, children, and smoking:* Not permitted. *Driving Instructions:* From Eugene, Oregon, take Route 126 west to Route 101 in Florence. Drive south 3 blocks to Maple Street and turn left.

## *Hood River, Oregon*

## COLUMBIA GORGE HOTEL

4000 Westcliff Drive, Hood River, OR 97031. 503-386-5566. *Innkeeper:* Lynne LaFountaine. Open all year.

Columbia Gorge Hotel is a striking villa built in 1921 by millionaire timber baron Simon Benson, Oregon's first tourism promoter. He spared no expense creating his "Waldorf of the West" on a scenic cliff high above the Columbia River, dwarfed by the backdrop of white-capped Mount Hood. The hotel is on 11 landscaped acres. A creek runs through the estate and drops 207 feet over Wah-Gwin-Gwin Falls to the gorge below.

In the lavish days of the Roaring Twenties, the hotel was considered *the* place to be seen, by both the landed gentry from the East and stars from California's newest industry, the movies. In a recent major restoration the imposing lobbies and dining room were decorated with antiques and reproductions designed to recapture the spell of the earlier era. Guest rooms were furnished with antiques of the period. Two suites feature fireplaces, and other rooms have king-size canopied beds. The hotel's restaurant, open to the public, is well known for its farm breakfasts, and reservations are a must!

The Columbia River, year-round skiing and mountain climbing at Mount Hood, and the sheer beauty of the Columbia River Gorge make this an exciting area to visit.

*Accommodations:* 42 rooms with private bath. *Smoking:* Restricted. *Driving Instructions:* The hotel is an hour east of Portland. Take exit 62 from I-84 (Westcliff Drive). Turn left on Westcliff to the hotel.

## *Jacksonville, Oregon*

### JACKSONVILLE INN

175 East California Street, Jacksonville, OR 97530. 503-899-1900.
*Innkeepers:* Linda and Jerry Evans. Open all year.

Jacksonville was Oregon's first Gold Rush town. One of the first permanent brick buildings in the boom town was the Jacksonville Hotel, constructed in 1861 of local bricks and hand-hewn sandstone from the local quarries and the old Jacksonville brick kiln.

The walls of the dining room are exposed sandstone, and the mortar still has flecks of gold glinting in it. Dinners are served by candlelight, and the highly acclaimed menu features fresh salmon (in season) and razor clams sautéed in butter. House specialties are veal dishes from old family recipes of the chef's and prime ribs au jus. The wine cellar contains more than seven hundred selections. A lounge with a bar adjacent to the restaurant.

The hotel's guest rooms are decorated with local antiques re-creating the colorful atmosphere of the old West. There are heavy oak bedsteads, antique brass beds, and dressers and rockers, surrounded by brick walls.

*Accommodations:* 8 rooms with private bath; 1 suite. *Driving Instructions:* From Medford, about 30 miles north of the California border on I-5, take Route 238 west 5 miles to Jacksonville.

## LIVINGSTON MANSION INN

4132 Livingston Road, Jacksonville, Oregon. Mailing address: Box 1476, Jacksonville, OR 97530. 503-899-7107. *Innkeeper:* Sherry Lossing. Open all year.

Livingston Mansion offers the best of two worlds: it sits on a hill surrounded by 4 acres of meadows, stately oaks, and madrona trees looking out over the Rouge Valley; and it is just a mile from the center of the historic town of Jacksonville. The warmth of one's reception here is due in great part to the Lossings' philosophy: "Remember to welcome strangers to our home, lest one might be an angel."

Well, breakfasts here are certainly heavenly. Guests gather on the patio or, in cool weather, by the fireside in the dining room. The table is set with a lacy tablecloth, family china, and a centerpiece of seasonal flowers. Along with juice and Oregon's famous peaches and pears, Sherry Lossing serves breakfast cookies, a family tradition chock full of raisins, nuts, and dried fruits. After this, a full breakfast with crepes or an egg dish is served – a perfect start to a day of rafting on the Rogue River.

The long, low English-style mansion was built in 1915 and features dark woods inside and out. An old wisteria spreads flower vines across the dark shingles and white trim of the bay windows and entrance. A swimming pool is set into the patio nearby.

Inside, soft Wedgwood blue and mauve combine with intense burgundy to provide the color scheme throughout the inn. Colors are coordinated in the wallpapers, fabrics, and comforters on the beds. The guest rooms, each differently decorated, share unsurpassed views of the valley, especially lovely at night when the lights twinkle like stars. Regal has its own fireplace and French doors leading to a private screened-in porch. Darkly stained wainscoting sets off the burgundy and blue paisley wallpaper. Amour is a bay-window room done in blues with a bedroom set imported from Belgium.

The Lossings, experts on the area, can steer guests to Jacksonville's many historic homes and buildings. Ashland's Shakespeare Festival, with performances from February through October, is just 12 miles away.

*Accommodations:* 5 rooms, 3 with private bath. *Pets and smoking:* Not permitted. *Driving Instructions:* Take the Medford exit off I-5 and go 5 miles west on Route 238.

## McCULLY HOUSE INN

240 East California Street, Jacksonville, Oregon. Mailing address: P.O. Box 13, Jacksonville, OR 97530. 503-899-1942. *Innkeeper:* Patricia Groth. Open all year; weekends only in winter.

This 1861 mansion, one of the six original dwellings erected here during Gold Rush days, is a good example of Classical Revival architecture. It was built by Dr. J.W. McCully, presumably to impress his wife, who had convinced the doctor to come to this boomtown. After rumors of her scandalous love affair reached him, however, Dr. McCully boarded a stagecoach and was never seen again. Jane carried on, raised a family, and opened her large home as a boardinghouse. Today, it has been fully restored. Several of the fine pieces now on display were original to the house, including the square baby grand in the parlor and a Renaissance Revival walnut bedroom suite, which were shipped around Cape Horn by Dr. McCully more than a century ago. The inn is decorated in a fresh, open style that combines elegant Victorian pieces with the clean lines of contemporary furniture, enhancing the rooms with greenery, polished oak floors, and attractive color schemes. Breakfast, lunch, and dinner are served in the dining room or on the outdoor patio and garden.

*Accommodations:* 3 rooms with private bath. *Pets and smoking:* Not permitted. *Driving Instructions:* From Medford, take Route 238 south 5 miles to California Street. The inn is at the corner of North Fifth.

## UNDER THE GREENWOOD TREE

3045 Bellinger Lane, Medford, OR 97501. 503-776-0000. *Innkeeper:* Renate Ellam. Open all year.

On a trip to Oregon, Renate Ellam found the Rogue Valley to be so irresistible that she bought herself a 125-year-old country farm and never looked back. The name "Under the Greenwood Tree" comes from a Shakespearean play, "As You Like It," and refers to a forest home of shepherds, milkmaids, and woodland peoples. Renate's inn offers orchards, gardens, farm animals, a rose garden, a gazebo, and acres of pasture and lawn. A willow swing awaits guests who just want to sit and relax. Bicycles are available, and there is a pick-up service for river rafters, fishermen, and skiers.

The inn was the farmhouse of the Walz Family who homesteaded here before century-old Medford became a town. Guests find Persian carpets, eclectic antiques, and an array of attractive quilts. Everyone gathers in the parlor for afternoon high tea and sherry. Three-course breakfasts are served in the dining room.

Each of the guest rooms is named for a variety of pear and features lace, needlepoint, chintz or velvets. Comice Room has a canopy bed and twig furniture in its sitting room, while Bartlett Room offers Chippendale furnishings and a sitting room of white wicker.

*Accommodations:* 2 rooms and 2 suites with private bath. *Pets and smoking:* Not permitted. *Children:* Under 13 not permitted. *Driving Instructions:* From I-5 take exit 27, Barnett Road, in Medford. Cross Barnett and turn onto Stewart Road heading southwest. Follow Stewart Road about 3 miles until it becomes Hull; continue one block and turn onto Bellinger Lane. The inn is on the left.

## *Mount Hood (Timberline), Oregon*

Mount Hood dominates the sky here. The 11,235-foot mountain was once an active volcano, and a climb to its summit will reveal a still-smoking crater. The mountain is Oregon's highest and provides year-round skiing and hiking. Several ski areas operate on the mountain.

### TIMBERLINE LODGE

Timberline Lodge, OR 97028. 503-231-7979; room reservations, 503-231-5400. *Innkeeper:* Richard L. Kohnstamm. Open all year. Timberline Lodge, the pride of Oregon, was one of Franklin D. Roosevelt's WPA Projects in the midst of the Depression; the president himself dedicated the building in 1937. As the name implies, it sits at the timberline (6,000 feet above sea level) on the slope of Oregon's highest mountain, Mount Hood. The lodge is a work of art; its mammoth structure with the 100-foot-high, 400-ton chimney stands as a proud testament to the Oregon men and women who built and furnished it. The chimney and fireplaces were fashioned out of volcanic rocks from the still-smoking Mount Hood. The lodge was constructed by hundreds of Oregonians who were taught stonemasonry, blacksmithing, carving, and building by local artisans and imported Old World craftsmen.

Throughout the lodge are works of art in a variety of media, all hand-crafted by local people from materials of the region. The heavy hardwood chairs and tables are hand-hewn and held together with iron straps and rugged rawhide seating. Telephone poles were sawed off and carved as newel posts for the stairways. The lodge maintains several themes in its varied decor. There are signs, carvings, paintings, weavings, metalwork, and stained glass depicting pioneers, Indians, and the wildlife of Oregon. The Blue Ox Bar on the lower level is decorated with stained-glass murals portraying Paul Bunyan and his ox, Babe. On the second floor is the Cascade Dining Room, heated by one of the inn's large fireplaces and serving three meals a day. There is a sauna and a large, heated outdoor swimming pool. In the Timberline complex is Wy'East Day Lodge, which houses all skier services.

Guest rooms are on several floors in the wings off the main section of the lodge. The furnishings and decor have an unusual strength and beauty in which the simplicity of the 1930s designs and the colorful hand-hooked rugs and appliqué bedspreads and drapes blend with the soft warmth of the blond woods. Richard Kohnstamm, the innkeeper for more than three decades, has, with many Oregon residents, organized "Friends of the Timberline." These "Friends" repair and replace worn furnishings with reproductions true to the original.

*Accommodations:* 53 rooms with private bath. *Pets:* Not permitted. *Smoking:* Restricted. *Driving Instructions:* From Portland take I-84 east for a short time, watching for signs to Route 26 at the Wood Village and Gresham exit. Stay on Route 26 going east to Government Camp. The lodge is 6 miles up the road from the Government Camp turnoff.

*Portland, Oregon*

## JOHN PALMER HOUSE

4314 North Mississippi Avenue, Portland, OR 97217. 503-284-5893.
*Innkeepers:* Mary and Richard Sauter. Open all year.

This 1890s house is a monument to the extravagance of the Victorian era, furnished throughout with many museum-quality antiques dating from the 1840s to the 1890s. Wallpapers are silk-screened with copper, silver, and gold inks. Ornate stained-glass windows and transoms, electrified gaslights, antique oil paintings, and silver and crystal complete the setting. Breakfasts, high tea, and five- to seven-course dinners are all available to the public by advance reservation, although tea and breakfast are complimentary for overnight guests.

Two guest rooms are in the main house, and three are in a cottage, which has a wraparound veranda. There is a spa available, and the innkeepers will arrange tours of the historic sections of Portland in their horse-drawn carriage.

*Accommodations:* 6 rooms, 2 with private bath. *Pets and smoking:* Not permitted. *Driving Instructions:* From I-5 take exit 303 and follow the Swan Island signs to Maryland Avenue. Turn left and drive 2 blocks to Skidmore. Turn left again, and drive 4 blocks to Mississippi.

*Seaside, Oregon*

## THE RIVERSIDE INN—BED AND BREAKFAST

430 South Holladay Drive, Seaside, OR 97138. 503-738-8254. *Innkeepers:* Sharon and Ken Ward. Open all year.

Seaside is a coastal resort town bustling with novelty and specialty shops, eateries, and a 2-mile-long promenade on its beach, running past classic old summer homes that dot the shore. Lewis and Clark's journey took them through this area, and the official "end of the trail" is nearby at the "Turnaround."

On the bank of the Necanicum River is a little motel-cum-inn, the Riverside. A 1950s motel and an adjoining 1907 home have been successfully transformed into a bower of wisteria and honeysuckle vines twining around windows and French doors decorated with oldfashioned latticework. The separate worlds of motels and inns blend nicely here: Guest rooms have private entrances and color television as well as old-fashioned country decor, with quilts, lace curtains, rocking chairs, and hanging plants. Guests gather in the parlor–library, where a European-style breakfast is served, including fresh fruit and baked goods. The backyard, filled with flowers, has a riverfront deck, a fine spot to relax, feed the ducks, and watch migrating salmon and steelheads on their journeys upstream. (A four-unit annex was added in 1986.)

*Accommodations:* 11 rooms with private bath. *Pets:* Not permitted. *Driving Instructions:* The inn is just off Route 101, 20 miles south of Astoria and 75 miles west of Portland.

## Steamboat, Oregon

### STEAMBOAT INN

Route 138, Steamboat, OR 97447. 503-498-2411. *Innkeepers:* Sharon and Jim Van Loan. Manager: Patricia Lee. Open all year.

From the outside, the Steamboat Inn looks for all the world like a truck stop. But behind the inn is the North Umpqua River. On its high bank are eight cabins—carpeted and knotty-pine paneled—with private baths. The cabins overlook the river and nestle among the towering firs of the Umpqua National Forest. Four additional cottages, not on the river, have lofts, fireplaces, and soaking tubs.

The water upstream from the Steamboat Inn is called the greatest stretch of steelhead fly water in North America. Anglers make pilgrimages here from all over the world to try their hand at fly fishing—the only method allowed on this 36-mile stretch of the river.

The main lodge serves as a fly shop, cafe, and dining room. The inn magically transforms itself in the evening about a half hour after sundown, when guests gather in the lodge by the stone hearth to enjoy the famous "fishermen's dinner." Candles and carafes of wine are set out on a table made from a single slab of sugar pine. Dinner, by advance reservation only, takes on an elegance accentuated by the rough-hewn surroundings.

*Accommodations:* 8 rooms and 4 cottages with private bath. *Pets and smoking:* Not permitted. *Driving Instructions:* The inn is 38 miles east of Roseburg on Route 138, 70 miles west of Crater Lake.

## WOLF CREEK TAVERN

Off I-5, Wolf Creek, Oregon. Mailing address: P.O. Box 97, Wolf Creek, OR 97497. 503-866-2474. *Innkeepers:* Sam and Joy Angelos. Open February through December.

Wolf Creek Tavern is a fine old stagecoach inn built along the north-south Oregon Territorial Road, the route of the California Stage Company's Portland-to-Sacramento line. It is an excellent example of this type of "tavern," as these roadside stops were called. The inn's main section, in the style of Classical Revival architecture, was built in the mid-nineteenth century. By 1922 the tavern had developed such a reputation for excellent food and lodging that the innkeepers constructed a wing to house more guests. The inn was popular with celebrities seeking peace and quiet — among them Jack London, who finished his "Valley of the Moon" here, with his wife, Charmian; Sinclair Lewis; Rutherford B. Hayes; Clark Gable, and Mary Pickford.

In 1975 the tavern was acquired by the Oregon State Parks and Recreation Department, and reconstruction and restoration began. Citizens of Wolf Creek and historians were consulted, and the inn began to regain its original appearance; the restoration also reflecting various periods in its evolution as a roadside inn from the nineteenth century to the present. The main section is furnished with nineteenth-century antiques, and the Dougall's wing has 1920s decor. On the first floor of the older section the ladies' parlor and the men's taproom (or lounge) are divided by the hall and central staircase. The fireplace in the men's section still bears the bootmarks left by weary travelers who stopped to warm their feet by the fireside. The dining room, formerly the inn's kitchen, serves meals to both guests and the public. The chalkboard menu features a variety of dishes and specializes in seafood.

Today, the inn has such amenities as heat, air-conditioning, and private guest baths. But as much as possible, the building, now listed in the National Register of Historic Places, retains its character as an inviting wayside stopover.

*Accommodations:* 8 guest rooms with private bath. *Pets:* Not permitted. *Smoking:* Restricted. *Driving Instructions:* The inn is 20 miles north of Grant's Pass, just off of I-5. From Roseburg, Oregon, take I-5 south 45 miles to exit 76. The inn is 1/2 mile from the exit from either the north or the south.

## FLYING M RANCH

23029 N.W. Flying M Ranch, Yamhill, OR 97148. 503-662-3222.
*Innkeepers:* Bryce and Barbara Mitchell. Open all year except
Christmas.

This inn, in a wilderness area surrounded by forested mountains that
extend to the coast, is on the old Yamhill–Tillamook stagecoach route
that crossed the mountains a century ago. In those days, weary travelers took food and shelter at Traveler's Home, an early hotel built here
by Mary and Joseph Petch. Local legend has it that a feuding com-
petitor ambushed and killed Mary and later poisoned himself rather
than face punishment.

In 1922, Bryce Mitchell's parents settled here, where later Bryce and
his sister were born. In 1957, Bryce brought his bride, Barbara, here
to live, and in 1970 the Flying M Ranch was born.

The log lodge houses dining rooms and a lounge, all decorated with
antique sawmill equipment and hunting trophies. A large stone fireplace dominates one room, and in cool weather fires burn in the hearth
around the clock. A six-ton Douglas fir log serves as a sturdy bar in
the lounge. The dining rooms, which offer Oregon country cooking
to overnight guests and the public, are open for breakfast, lunch, and
dinner. One dining room looks across the turf landing strip to a grassy
field where elk are often seen grazing at dusk. The landing strip makes
the ranch accessible to pilots and their families.

The ranch offers hayrides and trail rides that include overnight treks
to the sea, complete with steak cookouts over a trailside campfire. Back
at the ranch, a swimming hole the size of a city block awaits trail-weary
guests. The Flying M has a variety of accommodations, including guest
rooms in a building that is a cross between a motel and a bunkhouse.
A footbridge spans the river between the motel and the lodge. Seven
cabins and a number of rustic campsites complete the picture. The
honeymoon cabin has a fireplace and a Jacuzzi, and guests are treated
to fresh flowers and champagne.

*Accommodations:* 24 rooms and 7 cabins, each with private bath.
*Driving Instructions:* From Yamhill, drive 10 miles west on Moores
Valley Road and Oak Ridge Road. Follow the Flying M signs posted
on trees and fence posts.

# Washington

## *Anacortes, Washington*

### THE CHANNEL HOUSE

2902 Oakes Avenue, Anacortes, WA 98221. 206-293-9382. *Innkeepers:* Dennis and Pat McIntyre. Open all year.

Anacortes, known as the "gateway to the San Juan Islands," is a little island that is the hub of a ferry system that connects the islands of Puget Sound with Victoria, British Columbia. The Channel House overlooks Guemes Channel and the picturesque San Juans. Each guest room takes full advantage of the view. The shingled Victorian house was built in 1902 for an Italian count, and Pat and Dennis have furnished it with turn-of-the-century antiques. Guest rooms have brass, scrolly iron, or canopied beds. Rose cottage has two rooms, each with private bath and a fireplace. There is a second floor library-music room and a living room, each with a working fireplace. On the ground floor is the dining room, where fireside breakfasts are served. A favorite is the large hot tub in which guests can relax while watching the sun set over Puget Sound. Bicycles are available for exploring.

*Accommodations:* 6 rooms, 4 with private bath. *Pets and smoking:* Not permitted. *Children:* Under 12 not permitted. *Driving Instructions:* Take exit 230 off I-5 onto Route 20 West. Anacortes is twenty minutes west of Mount Vernon, Washington, which is about halfway between Seattle and Vancouver, Britist Columbia.

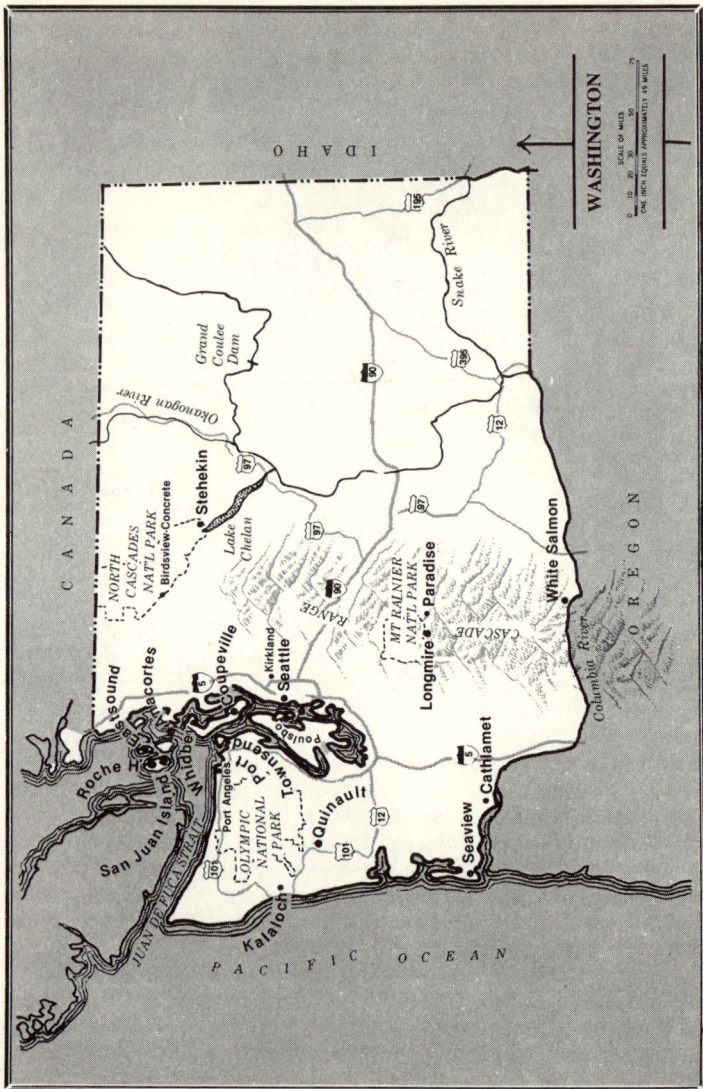

## NANTUCKET INN

3402 Commercial Avenue, Anacortes, WA 98221. 206-293-6007. *Innkeeper:* Sallie Lingwood. Open all year.

About the only thing commercial about Sallie Lingwood's Nantucket Inn is the name of the street on which it is found. As you enter the New England–style clapboard inn, you are immediately welcomed to the spacious parlor with its blue walls, country antiques, and fireplace. At the back of the house is Sallie Lingwood's kitchen with her wood-burning parlor stove. Upstairs, each bedroom is different, bearing her very personal touch. Sallie's favorite isn't the biggest or most expensive. It has an old French bed, an early English Duchess dresser, a pair of Mr.-and-Mrs. chairs, old-fashioned lamps, lace curtains, and a Karastan rug in soft hues. Sallie makes award-winning quilts in a thriving cottage industry. These appear folded at the foot of each guest's bed or hang on a quilt frame in the hall, ready to take the chill off a cool evening. Downstairs, books and magazines abound. The Nantucket Inn was built in 1925 as a fine home for a lumberman. It is every bit as enjoyable now.

*Accommodations:* 7 guest rooms, 1 with private bath and 1 with half bath. *Pets and smoking:* Not permitted. *Driving Instructions:* Anacortes is 16 miles west of Mount Vernon, Washington, on Route 20, which becomes Commercial Avenue.

*Bellingham, Washington*

## NORTH GARDEN INN

1014 North Garden, Bellingham, WA 98225. 206-671-7828. *Inn-keepers:* Barbara and Frank DeFreytas. Open all year.

This 1897 Queen-Anne Victorian, with rooms that are fresh and bright and with painted walls that display the DeFreytas' collection of North-western art, is on a hillside overlooking Bellingham Bay and the San Juan Islands. It is with a few blocks of Western Washington Universi-ty and just twenty minutes from British Columbia. The house retains the fine features that went into its construction, including unusual door knobs and hinges, a carved maple staircase, and many leaded- and stained-glass windows. Some guest rooms have water views. One has an old-fashioned fainting couch in front of a large round window. Breakfast includes fresh coffee and Barb's fresh-baked breads, pre-pared from her own home-ground flours.

*Accommodations:* 10 rooms, 2 with private bath. *Pets and smok-ing:* Not permitted. *Driving Instructions:* From I-5, take exit 253 and go west on Lakeway. At Ellis Street, bear right onto Holly and con-tinue to North Garden Street. Turn left and drive 2 1/2 blocks to the inn.

## Concrete-Birdsview, Washington

# CASCADE MOUNTAIN INN

3840 Pioneer Lane, Concrete-Birdsview, WA 98237. 206-826-4333.
*Innkeepers:* Ingrid and Gerhard Meyer. Open all year.

Ingrid and Gerhard Meyer fell in love with this wilderness area and decided to build a country inn so that others could enjoy it at a leisurely pace. The Skagit Valley of the Cascades offers hiking, fishing, river rafting, and hang gliding. Bird-watchers will appreciate the 1,500 acres of nearby national preserve that have been set aside for the hundreds of bald eagles that come here each year in search of migrating salmon.

The inn is a large barnlike structure with an international flavor and views of spectacular Sauk Mountain. The Meyers are natives of Germany, and they have decorated several of the guest rooms with artwork and feather quilts from their homeland. Other rooms reflect various cultures: One, in earthy tones, has many decorative pieces from Peru, as well as hand-woven Peruvian bedcovers; another is done in the tartan plaids and greens of Scotland. The living-room fireplace provides warmth for evening get-togethers, and in summer there are often singalongs around a campfire. Breakfast is served in the breakfast room or out on the patio. Lunch packs are available for hikers.

*Accommodations:* 6 rooms with private bath. *Pets and smoking:* Not permitted. *Children:* Under 10 not permitted. *Driving Instructions:* From Seattle, take I-5 north to Exit 230; then take Route 20 (North Cascades Highway) 24 miles east to Birdsview. Turn south on Wild Road and take the first right onto Pioneer Lane.

## Eastsound, Washington

### OUTLOOK INN

Main Street, Eastsound, Washington. Mailing address: P.O. Box 210, Eastsound, WA 98245. 206-376-2200. *Innkeeper:* Starr Farish. Open all year.

This wood-shingled inn, at the edge of the sea on this lovely island, has its own private beach, a small pond, and flower gardens. It was built as the local general store in the mid-1900s, and it housed the village jail in the rear. By 1888, the inn was operating as a guest house, when it served as a meeting place for the townspeople. Tradesmen who came to the island by steamer to buy fruit used to rely on the Outlook for home-style cooking and a clean room at the end of the pier.

The dining rooms serve breakfast, lunch, and dinner to overnight guests and the public. The inn's chef, from the Waldorf in New York, takes pride in the soups served at dinnertime. Favorites include garlic soup, carrot soup, and clam chowder. Dinner entrées vary nightly, but always include fresh fish flown to the island daily, fresh meats, vegetables, and flower-decorated salads. Drinks are available in a turn-of-the-century brass-railed bar.

The inn's old-fashioned rooms contain brass or hand-carved beds, marble-topped dressers, and collections of period memorabilia. Thirty addiitonal guest rooms are housed in two newer buildings constructed and furnished in keeping with the main inn.

*Accommodations:* 49 rooms. *Pets:* Inquire first. *Driving Instructions:* Take the ferry from Anacortes to Orcas. Drive north 8 miles to Eastsound and the inn.

## TURTLEBACK FARM INN

Crow Valley Road, Orcas Island, Washington. Mailing address: Route 1, Box 650, Eastsound, WA 98245. 206-376-4914. *Innkeepers:* Bill and Susan Fletcher. Open all year.

Turtleback Mountain can be seen from the Anacortes ferry as the boat approaches Orcas Island, where Turtleback Farm Inn overlooks Crow Valley. Set on eighty acres of meadows and forests, this former farmhouse has been restored and expanded to incorporate seven guest rooms with private baths, many of which have antique claw-footed tubs and pedestal sinks. Each room is named for its view; thus, Elm View overlooks the inn's old cork elm tree, while Meadow View, in the south wing, overlooks the fields. The innkeepers have decorated the inn with a blend of antiques and contemporary furniture.

The sitting room is a lively place in the evening, when guests gather to share their adventures over a glass of sherry or to play a game of Scrabble or cards. In the morning, the dining-room tables are set with bone china and crisp linens for a full breakfast of fresh eggs, meats, fresh juices, and fruit. In warm weather, breakfast is served on the sundeck. Turtleback Farm is central to all the island's offerings, including golf, charter boats, kayaking, fishing, and the peaceful countryside and sea. Many fine restaurants are nearby, and Susan and Bill will help guests plan an evening's outing or the next day's activities.

*Accommodations:* 7 rooms with private bath. *Pets and smoking:* Not permitted. *Children:* Over 8, by special arrangement. *Driving Instructions:* From the ferry, take Horseshoe Highway north. Take either the first or second left turn and then turn right on Crow Valley Road and drive north to the inn, on the right.

## MOON AND SIXPENCE

3021 Beaverton Valley Road, Friday Harbor, WA 98250. 206-378-4138. *Innkeepers:* Charles & Evelyn Tuller. Open all year. Moon and Sixpence is in the center of San Juan Island, with views of surrounding meadows, marshlands, and groves of firs. Built in 1906 as a dairy farm, guests are accommodated in the farmhouse and out-buildings. The inn welcomes cyclists, birders, hikers, and lovers of peace and tranquillity.

Evelyn, a weaver, has her studio/gallery in one of the outbuildings, and many rich textiles and antique fabrics from the Tullers' collections, as well as her own handiwork, have been used in decorating the inn. Family antiques from the mid-west and Pennsylvania Dutch country are also found throughout: The Navajo Den was named for its finely woven Navajo rugs; Island Suite has its own sitting room and reading nook; the Outpost is a one-room cottage with a Quaker flavor; and the old Water Tower has its own bath. The morning air is filled with the aroma of muffins baking and coffee brewing for breakfast.

*Accommodations:* 5 rooms, 1 with private baths. *Pets and smoking:* Not permitted. *Children:* Under 12 by special arrangement. *Driving Instructions:* From the Friday Harbor ferry slip, take Spring Street west to Second, continue to Guard Street, and bear right onto Beaverton Valley Road. The inn is about 3 miles from the ferry.

## SAN JUAN INN

50 Spring Street, Friday Harbor, Washington. Mailing address: P.O. Box 776, Friday Harbor, WA 98250. 206-378-2070. *Innkeepers:* Joan and Norm Schwinge. Open all year.

The San Juan Inn, 100 feet up the hill from the ferry dock and picturesque harbor, was built in 1873 and still retains the flavor of the Victorian West. Although it has the feeling of a turn-of-the-century establishment, it has been completely renovated, rewired, and replumbed.

The Schwinges completely furnished the place with Victorian antiques, adding little touches to give each room its special character. The bedrooms have old-fashioned bedsteads, some brass, others wicker. Some rooms overlook the harbor; others offer views of the patio gardens. The Schwinges added on a guest parlor with a wood-burning stove and a harbor view, where a complimentary breakfast is served. The back garden is a perfect place to sit and enjoy the harbor view and bask in the sun. Fresh flowers from the garden are often placed in guests' rooms. On winter evenings guests gather around the fire in the old parlor stove. The inn serves no regular meals, but several good restaurants within walking distance specialize in local seafood. Good fishing is available from nearby docks and charter boats.

*Accommodations:* 10 rooms with 3 shared baths. *Children:* Under 3 not permitted. *Driving Instructions:* Ferries leave Anacortes every few hours for the hour-and-fifty-minute cruise through the San Juan Islands to Friday Harbor. There is also a ferry from Sidney, British Columbia. Friday Harbor provides complete docking facilities for private boats and is served by three airlines.

*Ilwaco, Washington*

## INN AT ILWACO

120 Williams Street N.E., Ilwaco, WA 98624. 206-642-8686. *Owners:* The Blancher and Brewer families. *Innkeeper:* Jo Mueller and Don Ayers. Open all year.

The Ilwaco area was, for centuries, the summer camping grounds of the Chinook Indians. In 1805, Meriwether Lewis and William Clark arrived here with their expedition. Cape Disappointment is at the tip of the Long Beach peninsula, which has twenty-eight miles of beaches and two lighthouses. Ilwaco is a bed-and-breakfast hotel created from a former Presbyterian church. The Sunday school rooms on the second floor are now guest rooms, and the former church parlor is the setting for listening to music, having a cup of tea, or reading a book from the library. The former church sanctuary houses the Playhouse, a small performing arts theater where, in summer, a theater company and music groups perform. A full breakfast includes fresh-baked breads.

*Accommodations:* 9 rooms, 7 with private bath. *Pets and smoking:* Not permitted. *Driving Instructions:* From I-5, drive west on Route 101 and then south to the Long Beach Peninsula.

## Kalaloch, Washington

# KALALOCH LODGE

Route 101, Kalaloch, Washington. Mailing address: HC 80, Box 1100, Kalaloch Forks, WA 98331. 206-962-2271. *Manager:* Steve Dunn. Open all year.

Kalaloch is the handsomest of the concessioned overnight accommodations with Olympic National Park. The lodge is a sprawling, gray-shingled, two-story building that dates from 1952, when it was built to replace the 1925 original, which had burned. While most of the Olympic National Park is inland, a narrow strip runs 50 miles south from Ozette. It contains some of the most beautiful Washington coastline, including a fine beach with a sheltered lagoon.

This portion of the coastline was visited by the Washington Indian tribes, and the Northwestern Indian theme prevails in the interior of the lodge. The lobby is an rustic place with a stone fireplace. Overnight accommodations range from the original rooms in the lodge to a motel unit called Sea Crest House, containing modern rooms and suites with private baths and, in the three-room suites, fireplaces. Twenty-two log cabins have brass beds, free-standing fireplaces, and kitchenettes.

The Kalaloch dinner menu draws heavily from the local waters, including a shore dinner and local salmon, scallops, prawns, Pacific Northwest oysters, and cod fillets. Steak is also available.

*Accommodations:* 58 units with private bath. *Pets:* Permitted in the cabin area only; $10 fee. *Driving Instructions:* Kalaloch is directly on the coast on Route 101, 74 miles north of Aberdeen.

## SHUMWAY MANSION

11410 99th Place N.E., Kirkland, WA 98033. 206-823-2303. *Innkeepers:* Richard and Salli Harris and Julie Blakemore. Open all year.

Shumway Mansion, a four-story 1909 manor house rescued from the wrecker's ball by the Harrises, underwent a restoration that took almost four years and involved moving the building, the largest and oldest in the area, to its present site. The mansion's grounds include landscaped lawns, tall pines, and a natural ravine and rushing stream, less than a half hour from downtown Seattle. The porches, balconies, and many of the rooms overlook Lake Washington and Juanita Bay.

The inn's large rooms are furnished with turn-of-the-century antiques from Europe and America. On chilly days, fires burn in the hearths of the study and the living room. French doors lead to the Sun Room, where Salli and Richard provide a number of board games. A lakeside beach is three blocks from the inn, and athletic-club facilities are one block away. In addition to full breakfasts, beverages and seasonal snacks are served in the parlor each evening, and the inn's cookie jar always stands ready to assuage hunger pangs.

*Accommodations:* 7 rooms with private bath. *Pets and smoking:* Not permitted. *Children:* Under 13 not permitted. *Driving Instructions:* From I-405, take Exit 20A west to 99th Place, turn left, and drive 2 blocks to the inn.

## LaConner, Washington

### DOWNEY HOUSE BED AND BREAKFAST

1880 Chilberg Road, LaConner, WA 98257. 206-466-3207. *Innkeepers:* Kay and Jim Frey. Open all year.

The historic pioneer town of LaConner is on the Swinomish Channel, which separates LaConner from the Swinomish Indian Reservation. Hundreds of thousands of visitors come each spring to see the endless fields of blooming tulips during the Tulip Festival.

The Victorian Downey House was built by Peter Downey, a pioneer settler, at the turn of the century on a rise overlooking the Skagit Valley and the foothills of the Cascade Mountains. Guests are encouraged to relax and visit in the parlor, where a fire burns in the hearth each evening. Guest rooms are decorated with family antiques, comfortable Victorian farm pieces, and a collection of early historic photographs of the early pioneers.

Arriving guests are welcomed in the country kitchen, where Kay bakes her breakfast specialty—warm blackberry pie with lots of ice cream. Traditional breakfast fare is also available.

*Accommodations:* 5 rooms, 2 with private bath. *Pets and smoking:* Not permitted. *Children:* Under 10 not permitted. *Driving Instructions:* Take I-5 60 miles north from Seattle to exit 221 (LaConner). Drive west on Fir Island Road, crossing two separate forks of the Skagit River before coming to the inn, 6.6 miles from the exit.

PETER 1987

## THE WHITE SWAN GUEST HOUSE

1388 Moore Road, Mount Vernon, WA 98273. 206-445-6805. *Innkeeper:* Peter Goldfarb. Open all year.

White Swan was built as a private home in 1898 by the owner of the ferry boat service that carried passengers across the Skagit River. He included a turret on his new house so that he could watch the passing river traffic. Today, his lookout is a snug reading room.

The inn is decorated with overstuffed furniture, lace curtains, and a collection of samplers from the 1930s and 1940s. The porch is a comfortable spot to relax, and the wood-burning stove in the living room is a welcome source of warmth. There is always a plate of chocolate chip cookies set out for guests, while fresh coffee and muffins greet guests in the morning. The pastoral countryside is ideal for bicycling and bird-watching—the resident German Shepherd will accompany guests, if desired.

*Accommodations:* 3 rooms with 2 shared bath; 1 cottage. *Pets and smoking:* Not permitted. *Driving Instructions:* From I-5, take exit 221 and drive west 5 miles. At the yellow light, continue straight for 1 mile on Moore Road to the inn.

## Orcas Island, Washington

## ORCAS HOTEL

Ferry Landing, P.O. Box 155, Orcas, WA 98280. 206-376-4300. *Innkeeper:* Barbara Jamieson. Open all year.

The Orcas Hotel has stood on a rocky knoll overlooking the ferry landing on Orcas Island for more than eighty-five years, looking across the scenic waterways and San Juan Islands, which bear such names as Wasp Passage, Harney Channel, and Shaw Island. It is a short walk from Russell's Dock, so guest need not bring their car.

The restoration of the hotel, listed in the National Register of Historic Places, and its grounds was sanctioned by the National Parks Department. Photographs of the hotel's early days aided the Jamiesons with the restoration, as did conversations with a daughter of one of the hotel's earliest innkeepers.

Guest rooms are furnished much as they were at the beginning of this century, with the exception of the modern queen-size beds. Half the rooms share hall baths. Deluxe rooms have full baths with Jacuzzi tubs, French doors, and a semi-private deck. A few third-floor rooms have half-baths, although guests in these rooms use the hall showers. The hotel's full-service restaurant serves three meals daily. In season, the chef prepares dishes featuring freshly caught local seafood.

*Accommodations:* 12 rooms, 2 with private bath. *Pets:* Not permitted. *Smoking:* Restricted. *Driving Instructions:* From Seattle or Vancouver, take I-5 to Anacortes and follow signs to Anacortes Ferry. Guests with their own boats have complimentary mooring privileges at Russell's Dock.

*Port Angeles, Washington*

## TUDOR INN

1108 South Oak, Port Angeles, WA 98362. 206-452-3138. *Inn-keepers:* Jane and Jerry Glass. Open all year.

Tudor Inn is on a spacious lot with English-style gardens, overlooking the Strait of Juan de Fuca on one side and with a view of the Olympic Mountains on the other. Jane and Jerry Glass have decorated the fourteen-room, half-timbered, 1910 inn with many European antiques. On chilly days, the living room and the library always have fires in their hearths. A full breakfast of egg dishes, home-baked muffins and breads, jams, seasonal fruits, and pots of steaming hot coffee and tea is served in the dining room. Jane and Jerry offer special cross-country skiing weekends and will arrange weekend packages of snowshoeing or guided hikes around Lake Crescent or the Dungeness Spit. These weekends include Friday- and Saturday-night accommodations and all meals.

*Accommodations:* 5 rooms, 1 with private bath. *Pets, smoking, and children:* Not permitted. *Driving Instructions:* Take Highway 101 to Port Angeles. Continue west (the road becomes Lincoln Street) through the downtown section to 11th Street. Turn right and drive 2 blocks to the corner of Oak.

## HERITAGE HOUSE BED & BREAKFAST INN

305 Pierce Street, Port Townsend, WA 98368. 206-385-6800. *Innkeepers:* The Broughton and Ellis families. Open all year.

Heritage House is an 1880s Italianate Victorian on a bluff overlooking Port Townsend, the sparkling waters of the bay, and the Olympic mountain range. It has been restored and transformed by its two innkeeping families into a period piece where fine antiques and furnishings add to the atmosphere created by the building's architecture. Guest rooms, which offer views of the bay, mountains, and town, include Lily, a two-room suite that has a Victorian sitting room and a bedroom with a hand-carved four-poster bed. The three-piece Victorian bedroom set in Morning Glory has tiny flowers painted on the bed, while a volcano adorns the dresser. In other rooms, one may find brass-and-iron beds or patchwork quilts. Guests breakfast together in the dining room and in the evening gather in the parlor, where the innkeepers help them plan the next day's activities.

*Accommodations:* 6 rooms, 3 with private bath. *Pets and smoking:* Not permitted. *Children:* Under 9 not permitted. *Driving Instructions:* From Route 101, take Route 20 to Port Townsend. Go through the first light and take the first left onto Washington Street. Drive 5 blocks to the corner of Pierce Street.

## JAMES HOUSE

1238 Washington Street, Port Townsend, WA 98368. 206-385-1238. *Innkeepers:* Lowell and Barbara Bogart. Open all year.

Francis Wilcox James, a self-described "capitalist," spent $10,000 in 1889 on his home, in a day when most houses cost $2,000 or $3,000. James had been a customs agent, merchant, real estate dealer, and lighthouse keeper.

The inn is a triumph of Victorian splendor. The beautiful woods in the parquet floors and the banisters and wood trim, the elaborately carved period funiture, every mantelpiece, the wall coverings — all blend into a visual bouquet. Of the twelve guest rooms, the prize is the bridal suite, with fireplace, private bathroom, separate sitting room, and a balcony overlooking the bay. On the top floor are two additional rooms, which share two down-the-hall baths with showers, with views of the bay and either the Olympic or Cascade Mountains. The four second-floor bedrooms share two baths. On the lowest floor are a game

room and two garden suites, each with two bedrooms with two double beds, a bathroom, and a wood-burning stove or a fireplace. A garden cottage is also on the property.

Guests enjoy a breakfast of homemade muffins and coffee cakes served with coffee or tea and orange juice.

*Accommodations:* 12 rooms, 4 with private bath. *Pets and smoking:* Not permitted. *Driving Instructions:* From Seattle, take a ferry to Winslow, drive to Port Townsend. From Vancouver, go down to Whidbey Island and across on the Keystone Ferry. From Olympia, take U.S. 101 around the Hood Canal.

## LINCOLN INN

538 Lincoln Street, Port Townsend, WA 98638. 206-385-6677. *Innkeepers:* Joan and Robert Allen. Open February through December 20th.

Lincoln Inn was built by Port Townsend's master builder George Starrett in 1888. This brick-faced Victorian was constructed for a mason, Elias De Voe, who wanted his home to be an advertisement for his brick company. The Allens have restored and preserved many of the architectural features of the house, including its moldings, large sliding double doors, and kerosene chandeliers. Joan and Robert have decorated the Lincoln with an eye to creating a romantic setting, furnishing rooms with antiques, many brought here by early settlers. Old-fashioned English floral-print wallpapers and antique Persian rugs are set off by polished wood floors, and private tiled bathrooms still have their original claw-footed tubs and antique fixtures. On chilly evenings, the Allens keep a fire in the parlor hearth, where complimentary glasses of sherry and wine are offered. Breakfast and dinner are served in the dining room on fine china and silver. The inn is especially popular with guests on honeymoons or celebrating anniversaries. The innkeepers provide bicycles for guests, an ideal way to tour this Victorian village.

*Accommodations:* 3 rooms with private bath. *Pets and children:* Not permitted. *Smoking:* Restricted to the parlor. *Driving Instructions:* In Port Townsend, take Water Street to the end and turn left on Monroe. Drive 5 blocks up the hill to Lincoln and turn left.

## LIZZIE'S

731 Pierce Street, Port Townsend, WA 98368. 206-385-4168. *Innkeepers:* Bill and Patti Wickline. Open all year.

Lizzie was the wife of Captain Thomas Grant, an intermittently prosperous seafarer and shipowner. In 1887, she bought the land here and built a handsome Italianate Victorian home with double bay windows, 12-foot ceilings, painted interior moldings, and ornate mantels. The many Victorian antiques are of a scale possible only in a house of this size.

The inn's front parlor retains its 1887 Parisian wall and ceiling papers. On the floor is rich red wall-to-wall carpeting topped here and there with Oriental throw rugs. Originally the dining room, the inn's drawing room has a second fireplace with the original overmantel. A leather Victorian chesterfield and comfortable armchairs are gathered around the fire.

The master bedroom has a fireplace and private bath. Other rooms,

some named for earlier inhabitants of the house, include Daisy's Room, which still bears the autograph she wrote on the wall in 1894. From Daisy's window, you can watch the sun come up over the bay. In Sarah's room, bay-window seats overlook the sound and the mountains. Lizzie's combines spectacular views with the personal attentiveness of its innkeepers.

*Accommodations:* 8 rooms, 4 with full bath and 1 with half bath. *Pets:* Not permitted. *Children:* Under 10 not permitted. *Driving Instructions:* From Route 20, drive to the first traffic light in town. Turn left at Kearney, go 2 blocks, turn right at Lawrence, and continue 5 blocks. Turn left at Pierce, where the inn is on the left.

## MANRESA CASTLE

Seventh and Sheridan, Port Townsend, Washington. Mailing address: P.O. Box 564, Port Townsend, WA 98368. 206-385-5750. *Innkeeper:* Jill Tomasi. Open all year.

The year is 1892 and Port Townsend is a booming community. Real estate values are soaring, and the lumber business is bringing more and more residents. Charles Eisenbeis has come to town to make his fortune in crackers and brewing, a nicely dovetailed pair of businesses. Nothing will do but the best house in the town for his young bride, and nothing to be found suits the aspiring lord of the manor. So he sets out to build a castle in keeping with his means. Scanning the countryside, he selects the highest point in the area and constructs a turreted castle reminiscent of his native Prussia. The mansion is elegant and possesses a commanding view of the entire town, Puget Sound, and both the Olympic and Cascade mountain ranges. Unluckily for Eisenbeis, the boom period quickly declines, and he is forced to abandon the castle. The castle is sold to the Jesuit order of clergy, who maintain it as a school until the late 1960s, when Ronald and Carol Smith buy the 30,000-square-foot castle and set out to restore the elegance that had long since disappeared. In the process they restore the guest rooms and numerous hallways and parlors. To the original structure they fit color-cable television sets, room phones, and private bathrooms, so that most overnight guests can appreciate the old-fashioned splendor without forgoing modern conveniences.

The castle today is filled with antiques, including scrolly beds, handsome chests, period-style lights, swagged curtains, elaborate carved sideboards, dark wood trim around doors and windows, luxurious carpeting, and overstuffed furniture. The effect is opulent, but not offensively so. The opulence is fun, and, after all, it *is* a castle.

The dining room at the inn is set with linen, has bentwood chairs, and offers a selection of Northwestern seafood, steaks, and prime rib.

*Accommodations:* 40 rooms with private bath. *Pets:* Not permitted. *Driving Instructions:* Take either U.S. 101 (the Olympic Loop Highway) or Route 104 to Route 20, which leads to Port Townsend. As you enter Port Townsend, the Castle is one block north of Route 20 on Sheridan Avenue.


## STARRETT HOUSE INN

744 Clay Street, Port Townsend, WA 98368. 206-385-3205. *Innkeepers:* Bob and Edel Sokol. Open all year.

Starrett House, one of the most photographed mansions of the Pacific Northwest, is a fanciful Victorian replete with gables, gingerbread, 14-foot frescoed ceilings, chandeliers, and a tower, which has a free-hanging 2-story staircase, identified by the Smithsonian Institute to be the only one of its type in this country. Frescoes in the tower depict the seasons of the year.

All rooms are furnished with antiques. The drawing room overlooks Puget Sound and the Olympic Mountains; the bay can be seen from the master bedroom; and Nanny's Room offers a view of the Cascade Mountains and Puget Sound. A full complimentary breakfast, and dinner is served in the dining room or on china and crystal in guests' rooms.

*Accommodations:* 9 rooms, 7 with private bath; 1 guest house. *Pets and smoking:* Not permitted. *Children:* Under 13 not permitted. *Driving Instructions:* Take Route 20 through the business district to Monroe Street. Turn left and take the second left onto Clay Street.

## MANOR FARM INN

26069 Big Valley Road N.E., Poulsbo, WA 98370. 206-779-4628.
*Innkeepers:* Robin and Jill Hughes. Open all year.

An hour from Seattle, this inn is an idyllic country place where old-fashioned roses twine around porch posts, a proud rooster struts the manicured grounds, sheep graze in the pastures, dappled sunlight filters through the leaves, and mountain breezes freshen the air. At the heart of all this, the white turn-of-the-century farmhouse and its more recent additions form a sheltered courtyard around lawn and gardens.

Robin and Jill Hughes purchased their thirty-acre farm in 1975 and have created a haven to be shared with guests. The inn has English and French pine antiques, working fireplaces encircled by comfortable seating, and open-beamed ceilings. Windows and French doors look out on English-style gardens and pastures. The sitting room echoes the understated mood with upholstered furniture and an old pine side table set with a bouquet of garden flowers. In the evening, guests gather in this room for a glass of sherry and then join the public at dinner in the small dining room with its wood-burning hearth and fresh flowers. The menu, a single-entrée chef's choice, usually features regional seafoods. Farm breakfasts are served.

*Accommodations:* 8 rooms 6 with private bath; 2 cottages. *Pets, smoking, and children:* Not permitted. *Driving Instructions:* From Seattle, take the Winslow Ferry to Bainbridge Island. Take Route 305 north to Route 3, turn right, and drive about 4 miles north to Big Valley Road. Turn right; the inn is about 1 mile on the right.

Quinault is on the fringes of the Olympic National Forest, which borders the Olympic National Park. The surrounding region is rain forest. The area receives more than 12 feet of rain annually.

## LAKE QUINAULT LODGE

South Shore Road, P. O. Box 7, Quinault, WA 98575. 206-288-2571.
*Innkeepers:* ARA Leisure Services. Open all year.

Although there has been a log hotel on the site since the 1890s to accommodate those coming to Lake Quinault, it was not until 1926 that the main lodge was built. Frank McNeil had visited the Quinault rain forest area on his vacations from the *Seattle Post-Intelligencer*, where he was a Linotype operator. He acquired a special permit from the U.S. Forest Service to build and operate a lodge and then enlisted the financial support of a wealthy lumberman and mill operator named Ralph Emerson. They selected a site that would provide a view of the lake and began the difficult process of construction. All the materials for the tremendous undertaking had to be hauled over 50 miles of dirt road, and the transportation process was kept up for twenty-four hours a day. A large crew of local and imported craftsmen was hired to put up the hotel, and they accomplished the almost impossible by completing the task in just ten weeks from start to finish.

As one enters the lobby, the great care taken in workmanship is immediately evident from the heavy-beamed wood ceilings to the bank of small-paned windows that flanks the brick fireplace dominating one wall. The room is carpeted, and the large collection of wicker furniture is part of the original collection that McNeil and Emerson installed. The main lodge, with its handsome stenciled ceilings, is much like a baronial country manor and is the most innlike part of the resort. The forest room is rustic in appearance and contains the main cocktail lounge and bar. The dining room, whose bank of picture windows reveals a panoramic view of the lake below, stresses seafood and also serves à la carte breakfast and luncheon.

Overnight accommodations range from the old-fashioned comfort of the 1920s-style rooms with their claw-footed tubs to those which are more modern. All of this was more than good enough for President Franklin Roosevelt when he visited in 1937. He was so inspired

that he was moved to create Olympic National Park the following year.

There is much to do amid the "no-need-to-do-anything" atmosphere of the rain-forest surroundings. The U.S. Forest Service offers hikes in the rain-forest. The lodge offers swimming in its large indoor pool; a Jacuzzi whirlpool; men's and women's saunas; a lakefront dock with paddle boats; a recreation room with table tennis, pool table, and a number of modern electronic games; and plenty of trails for hiking. Fishing opportunities are plentiful, with cutthroat, rainbow, and Dolly Varden trout the most frequent prizes. Winter-run steelhead fishing is good in local rivers. The lake is part of the Quinault Indian Reservation, and a special license must be obtained from the tribe for a fee before non-Indians may fish there.

*Accommodations:* 56 rooms with private bath. *Pets:* Pets are subject to a size limit and restricted to certain areas. *Smoking:* Annex only. *Driving Instructions:* Quinault is located about 40 miles north of Aberdeen on Route 101. At Quinault, take South Shore Road to the lodge.

## San Juan Island, Washington

# HOTEL DE HARO: ROCHE HARBOR RESORT

San Juan Island, Washington. Mailing address: P.O. Box 4001, Roche Harbor, WA 98250. 206-378-2155. *Innkeeper:* Neil J. Tarte. Open all year.

The Hotel de Haro is set amid beautiful formal flower gardens and overlooks the sheltered harbor and the islands beyond. The original 1845 trading post, forming the heart of the hotel, was expanded in 1886 to a hotel-resort for visiting businessmen in the limestone industry.

Three-story verandas wrap around the white-painted wooden building, and ivy twines up and around the railings and pillars. In the foyer is a large fireplace kept burning throughout the cooler months. The guest rooms contain eclectic period furnishings, mostly original to the hotel. The Presidential Suite, used by Roosevelt and William Howard Taft, has its own working fireplace and private veranda. The front rooms open onto the verandas, which have views of the harbor.

The restaurant features seafood straight from local waters. When the weather is cold, the restaurant is open on weekends only. The big outdoor heated swimming pool and the tennis courts are available to guests. The marina at the hotel's doorstep offers full boating facilities and rentals.

*Accommodations:* 20 guest rooms; 4 are suites with private baths, 16 rooms share 4 hall baths. 7 cottages and 45 condominiums are also on the property. *Pets:* Not permitted. *Driving Instructions:* Take the Anacortes Ferry to San Juan. Then take Roche Harbor Road 9 miles to the resort. Private planes can land on the 4,000-foot airstrip here. Boats dock at the extensive facilities in the harbor.

*San Juan Island, Washington*

## OLYMPIC LIGHTS

4531A Cattle Point Road, Friday Harbor, WA 98250. 206-378-3186.
*Innkeepers:* Lea and Christian Andrade. Open all year.

Olympic Lights is surrounded by vast grassy meadows that descend gently to the sea. The Olympic Mountains rise majestically across the Strait of Juan de Fuca. At night the lights of Victoria twinkle across the water.

The farmhouse was built in 1895 on 350 acres, although only five acres remain today. Rooms are spacious and airy, decorated with contemporary pieces, a small selection of antiques, wall-to-wall carpeting, and pastel colors. After a day of biking and exploring the island, guests may relax by the fire in the parlor and enjoy a glass of sherry. Mornings begin with a farm breakfast prepared with eggs contributed by the resident chickens. The American Camp, a National Park, is just down the road.

*Accommodations:* 5 rooms, 1 with private bath. *Pets and smoking:* Not permitted. *Driving Instructions:* Take the ferry from Anacortes to Friday Harbor. There is courtesy transportation from the ferry to the inn.

## BEECH TREE MANOR

1405 Queen Anne Avenue North, Seattle, WA 98109. 206-281-7037.
*Innkeeper:* Virginia Lucero. Open all year.

Beech Tree Manor is a 1904 mansion named for the impressive copper beech tree on its grounds. The manor is centrally located in the historic district of Queen Anne Hill, from which trolleys link the inn with downtown Seattle. Virginia Lucero has decorated the spacious rooms around an English country theme, with floral wallpapers, antique lace, and English antique furnishings, and original contemporary artwork in all the guest rooms. Dark paneling downstairs sets off the delicate floral patterns of the upholstered furniture and drapes, and a forty-foot-long library has hand-embossed tin wall-coverings above its paneling, decorative touches that create a mood reminiscent of a British manor house. In the morning, a sumptuous breakfast is served. Virginia has an antique and linen-and-lace shop at the inn.

*Accommodations:* 6 rooms, 3 with private baths. *Pets and smoking:* Not permitted. *Children:* Under 6 not permitted. *Driving Instructions:* Take I-5 to Denny Avenue and drive west to First Avenue North. Turn right and drive to Roy; turn left and drive to Queen Anne Avenue North. Turn right to the inn.

## CHAMBERED NAUTILUS BED & BREAKFAST INN

5005 22nd Avenue N.E., Seattle, WA 98105. 206-522-2536. *Innkeepers:* Bunny and Bill Hagemeyer. Open all year.

At the Chambered Nautilus, a blue Georgian–Colonial-style house built in 1915 on a steep hillside, has a garden setting and views of the Cascade Mountain range that belie its city locale. Palladian French doors open onto the roof of the front entrance portico. Inside, the inn is furnished with English and American antiques, Oriental rugs, and a grand piano. The guest rooms are on the second and third floors; all are decorated differently, and all but have their own porches. Guests may relax and visit by the fireside in the parlor and enjoy a cup of tea. The full breakfast includes apple quiche, blueberry "serene scene," French toast with homemade syrups, basil scrambled eggs on cheese toast, and fresh fruits and juices.

*Accommodations:* 6 rooms with shared baths. *Pets and smoking:* Not permitted. *Children:* Under 12 not permitted. *Driving Instructions:* From I-5 north in downtown Seattle, take exit 169 (N.E. 50th — University of Washington). Turn right at the light and then left at 20th Avenue N.E. Drive 4 our blocks and turn right at N.E. 54th, go 2 blocks, and turn right on 22nd Ave. N.E.

## THE COLLEGE INN GUEST HOUSE

4000 University Way N.E., Seattle, WA 98105. 206-633-4441. *Innkeepers:* Jim & Judy Oliver. Open all year.

In 1909, a group of businessmen decided to hold a world's fair to be known as the Alaska–Yukon Pacific Exposition, to introduce to the world the products of the Northwest, the Pacific, Hawaii, Japan, and China. To increase the city's hotel capacity, the College Inn was constructed. Today, the timbered, Tudor-style gabled building serves as the city's most well-known European-style small hotel, which is listed in the National Register of Historic Places.

Pictures of the 1909 exposition hang on the entryway's brick and paneled walls. A stairway leads to three floors of the inn's guest and public rooms above. Each guest room has been refurbished simply with wall-to-wall carpeting, in-room sinks, and a combination of antique and newer bedsteads.

On the fourth floor, in the gabled attic, is the inn's sitting room, with period furnishings and an ever-present supply of coffee or tea. A Continental breakfast is served here each morning. The ground floor houses a café, a pub, and a delicatessen.

*Accommodations:* 25 rooms with shared baths. *Pets:* Inquire first. *Driving Instructions:* Take I-5 to the N.E. 45th Street exit. Drive east to to 15th Avenue, then drive south to N.E. 40th.

## GALER PLACE

318 West Galer Street, Seattle, WA 98119. 206-282-5339. *Innkeepers:* Chris and Terry Giles. Open all year.

Christine's green thumb has transformed this 1906 home into a bower of greenery. The vegetable and flower gardens in the enclosed backyard are surround the redwood deck. No detail was spared in restoring this in-town bed-and-breakfast guest house. Chris brings several years' innkeeping experience with her from her native Great Britain.

The four guest rooms are furnished with antiques befitting the age and dignity of the house. One has its own loft-sitting room. A generous full breakfast is served in the dining room, and afternoon tea is an enjoyable gathering in the plant-filled parlor. Galer Place is with walking distance of Seattle Center and the Opera House and is on Metro Transit line number 2, which provides transportation to downtown attractions including Pike Place Market.

*Accommodations:* 4 rooms with private bath. *Smoking:* Not permitted. *Children:* Under 10 not permitted. *Driving Instructions:* Driving north on I-5, take the Seneca Street exit to First Avenue, turn right and go across Denny Way to Roy Street. Turn left and continue 1 block to Queen Anne Avenue North. Turn right and follow Queen Anne to the top of the hill, turn left on Galer, and drive three blocks to the inn.

## ROBERTA'S BED AND BREAKFAST

1147 16th Avenue East, Seattle, WA 98112. 206-329-3326. *Innkeeper:* Roberta C. Barry. Open all year.

Roberta's, in Seattle's historic Capitol-Hill neighborhood, is a turn-of-the-century home with a balustraded front porch decorated with potted greenery. Guest rooms are furnished with antiques and comforters. Madrona Room has a big oak bed, while Plum Room, with queen-size beds, has room for an extra guest in its loft bed. Breakfast is served at a communal table. The inn is with walking distance of many of Seattle's attractions. The Art Museum and Conservatory is close.

*Accommodations:* 4 rooms, 2 with private bath. *Pets and smoking:* Not permitted. *Children:* Under 13 not permitted. *Driving Instructions:* The inn is five minutes east of downtown, 1 block east of Volunteer Park.

## WILLIAMS HOUSE BED & BREAKFAST INN

1505 Fourth Avenue North, Seattle, WA 98109. 206-285-0810. *Innkeepers:* Susan and Doug Williams. Open all year.

Susan and Doug Williams have created an oasis of warmth and turn-of-the-century elegance. The 1905 Edwardian-era house — on Queen Anne hill overlooking Seattle's skyline, the Cascade Mountains, Mount Rainier, and the sparkling waters of Puget Sound — is just blocks from Seattle Center and the Space Needle and a mile from the center of downtown Seattle.

The inn retains some of its original wall-coverings and gas lighting fixtures, and the innkeepers have furnished it with many formal Victorian pieces. Filmy curtains at the large bay windows filter the light that brightens the rooms. Four of the guest rooms have commanding views of the area, while the fifth offers peaceful privacy. One particularly spacious room has sunny bay windows, original wall-coverings, and a half-testered bed. The living room, with its marble-topped tables and lavish parlor suite, is a favorite gathering spot.

*Accommodations:* 5 rooms, 2 with private bath. *Pets and smoking:* Not permitted. *Driving Instructions:* From I-5, take the Mercer-Fairview exit and follow signs to Seattle Center (Space Needle). Turn right onto Fifth Avenue and then left onto Highland. Drive 2 blocks to the stop sign, turn right onto Third, drive 2 blocks to Galer, turn right, and drive 1 block to the corner of Fourth Avenue North.

## Seaview, Washington

### THE SHELBURNE INN AND RESTAURANT

Pacific Highway 103 and 45th Street, Seaview, Washington. Mailing address: P.O. Box 250, Seaview, WA 98644. 206-642-2442. *Innkeepers:* Laurie Anderson & David Campiche. Open all year.

The Shelburne Inn is a restoration of a Victorian hostelry built in 1896. Now in the National Register of Historic Places, it was built by Charles Beaver as an overnight rest stop for travelers on an old sidewheeler, the *T. J. Potter,* out of Portland.

The innkeepers have carefully restored the Shelburne inside and out, returning it almost perfectly to its original state. The interior is completely covered with warm dark woods of the original tongue-and-groove fir. The decor is Victorian, with English and American antiques. The lobby has a large fireplace surrounded by comfortable sofas, love seats, and period pieces. Guest rooms are furnished in keeping with the inn's vintage. There are brass beds, heavy oaken dressers, walnut bedroom suites, and graceful, scrolly iron-and-brass bedsteads with accents of antique quilts, and lacy white curtains.

The Shelburne's restaurant, Shoalwater, has received national acclaim under the separate ownership of Ann and Tony Kischner, who offer imaginative seafood dishes, quail, veal, and pasta. Full breakfasts are served to guests. An English-style pub has been added recently.

*Accommodations:* 16 rooms, 13 with private bath. *Pets:* Not permitted. *Driving Instructions:* Take Pacific Highway (Route 103) into Seaview.

## South Cle Elum, Washington

### THE MOORE HOUSE BED & BREAKFAST

526 Marie, South Cle Elum, Washington. Mailing address: P.O. Box 2861, South Cle Elum, WA 98943. 509-674-5939. *Innkeepers:* Monty and Connie Moore. Open all year.

Moore House Inn, built at the turn of the century originally to house crews working on the railroad, is a refurbished railway hotel nestled in the Cascade Mountains of Central Washington. Guest rooms, each named for one of the men who once stayed here, have ruffled lace curtains, flowered comforters, and floral print wallpapers, as well as dust ruffles, hand-sewn decorative pillows, and historic photographs and railroad memorabilia. The railroad theme continues in the yard, where a caboose is has been renovated to provide additional rooms. The property is bordered by a creek, and the inn has views of the nearby mountains. In winter, the Moores offer sleigh rides and cross-country skiing from the front door. In summer, covered wagon trips traverse part of the adjacent 14-mile Iron Horse Trail.

*Accommodations:* 11 rooms, 5 with private bath. *Pets:* Not permitted. *Smoking:* Lobby only. *Driving Instructions:* From I-90, take the South Cle Elum exit to Madison and follow the signs to the inn.

*Spokane, Washington*

## WAVERLY PLACE BED & BREAKFAST

West 709 Waverly Place, Spokane, WA 99205. 509-328-1856. *Innkeepers:* Marge and Tammy Arndt. Open all year except Christmas. Waverly Place is a Queen-Anne Victorian — all turrets, gables, and verandas — across the street from the eleven-acre Corbin Park, which was originally built as a sulky track for harness racing and is now a favorite loop for joggers and walkers. The inn has its original gas chandeliers and beaded woodwork and wainscotting. There are two living rooms, one with a library, a fireplace, and a window seat. The other is more formal, with Victorian parlor furnishings. Skinner Suite has a large brass-and-enamel bed and is decorated in a country motif. The highlight of Anna's Room is an oval, leaded-glass window and window seat. Garden Room has vines and flowers stenciled on the walls.

Tea and cookies are served by the fireside in winter, with cookies and lemonade the requisite fare in summer. Tammy and Marge Arndt prepare a breakfast that includes such specialties as sunrise tomatoes, eggs baked inside herbed tomatoes accompanied by Swedish coffee cake, or Swedish pancakes with homemade huckleberry sauce.

*Accommodations:* 3 rooms, 1 with private bath. *Pets:* Not permitted. *Smoking:* Living room only. *Driving Instructions:* From I-90, take the Newport Highway exit and go north on Division Street to Waverly Place. Turn west onto Waverly Place and drive past Corbin Park to the inn, at the corner of Wall.

## Whidbey Island, Washington

# THE CAPTAIN WHIDBEY

2072 Captain Whidbey Inn Road, Coupeville, WA 98239. 206-678-4097. *Innkeeper:* Captain John Colby Stone. Open all year. Here is a fine turn-of-the-century log structure, listed in the National Register of Historic Places, with more warmth than you might imagine possible. The inn is a two-story, twin-roofed building constructed of perfectly fitted peeled madrona logs, popular with Judge Lester Still, who built the inn at the edge of Penn Cove in 1907.

Furnishings throughout the inn reflect the comfort of the turn of the century, with original or reproduction lighting, overstuffed furniture, and antique occasional pieces. The windows have small panes. Public rooms include the living room with its broad stone fireplace and early, almost primitive paintings. The Chart Room is an informal bar–lounge with a dart board and a Franklin stove. The dining room, under Chef James Horvath, features northwestern cuisine.

Accommodations outside the main building include rooms with fireplaces in several cottages and an annex with rooms overlooking the lagoon. Many will prefer the rooms in the main inn for their historic feeling, though they share hall bathrooms. Captain Stone takes guests on sailing charters on Penn Cove.

*Accommodations:* 30 rooms, 17 with private bath. *Pets:* Permitted in cottages only. *Smoking:* Restricted. *Driving Instructions:* The inn is in Penn Cove, 2 1/2 miles north of Coupeville on Whidbey Island. Go to Penn Cove via Route 20 from the north or Route 525 from the south.

# THE SARATOGA INN

4850 South Coles Road, Langley, WA 98260. 206-221-7526. *Innkeeper:* Debbie Jones. Open all year.

The Saratoga Inn is perched atop a hill overlooking the Saratoga Passage, the strait between Whidbey Island and the mainland to the east. In the distance can be seen the Cascade Mountains. The inn is a Cape Cod–style house with wooded sunbursts set into its gables and with beveled windows flanking its blue paneled doors. Pots of seasonal flowers and other plants add a welcoming touch to the entrance. Twenty-five acres of meadows and forests surround the Saratoga Inn, which, although it looks as if it's been here awhile, was built in 1982.

The inn has many special characteristics that help make up a fine country inn: wildflower-covered meadows, nearness to the sea, scenic views, bright, airy rooms, and country antiques. Each guest room has its own unique feature. Country Garden offers sea views by a fireside. Meadow faces southwestward, offering sunsets and meadow vistas. Willow, with its bent-willow bed and rocker, has a Franklin stove on a brick hearth. Queen Anne's Lace looks out across Puget Sound.

Mornings are a treat, with complimentary home-baked muffins served with Debbie's jams and jellies. In the afternoons guests can stroll in the gardens or relax in the tree house.

*Accommodations:* 5 rooms with private bath. *Pets, smoking, and children:* Not permitted. *Driving Instructions:* From downtown Seattle drive north on I-5 to the Whidbey Island–Mukilteo Ferry exit (exit 189). Proceed to Mukilteo, take a ferry to Whidbey Island, and follow the signs to Langley. From the north cross the Deception Pass Bridge on Route 20 and take Route 525 south to Langley.

## VICTORIAN HOUSE

602 North Main Street, Coupeville, Washington. Mailing address: P.O. Box 761, Coupeville WA 98239. 206-678-5305. *Innkeeper: Dolores Fresh.* Open all year.

Victorian House, just four blocks from the waterfront, is an Italianate townhouse built in 1889 for the Jenne family, who operated a hotel in town. Now listed in the National Register of Historic Places, the inn was considered avant garde in its day: It had built-in closets and an ingenious system that gathered rain water, which was then pumped to a tower—thus providing the first running water on the island. The hot-water heating system, then the talk of the town, still warms the house today. The trees in the old orchard continue to provide cherries, plums, and apples.

Guests may relax in the parlor, on the porch, or out in the orchard. Upstairs, two corner rooms provide accommodations. Breakfast is served in the dining room.

*Accommodations:* 2 rooms with private bath; 1 cottage suite with kitchen. *Pets and smoking:* Not permitted. *Children:* Under 12 not permitted. *Driving Instructions:* Coupeville is on Whidbey Island. The inn is on Main Street, in the center of town.

## INN OF THE WHITE SALMON

Route 14, White Salmon, Washington. Mailing address: P.O. Box 1446, White Salmon, WA 98672. 509-493-2335. *Innkeeper:* Sheryl Fletcher. Open all year.

When the local hotel burned down in the mid-1930s, White Salmon businessman Bill Lauterback engaged European craftsmen to build a replacement. Thirty years later, the "new" hotel was bought and transformed into an inviting bed-and-breakfast inn, replete with Victorian wallcoverings and a nice collection of antique furnishings. In the honeymood suite, the Victorian dresser has an attached tilting mirror and displays, on the top, a number period accessories such as a lace dresser scarf, an antique hand mirror, and a pin bowl. In other rooms, there are lacy pincushions and antique shaving mugs and brushes. Brass beds are the rule.

Breakfast features breads and pastries, some filled with cheese and served hot with nut and caramel sauce. Juices, fruits, and eggs are also available regularly. During Washington's bountiful fruit season, large bowls of berries or plates of sliced melons are put out. In winter, hot oatmeal with cream and brown sugar is served.

The inn is popular in the winter thanks to cross-country skiing at Trout Lake, at the base of Mount Adams. After a day of skiing, guests can return to enjoy resful soaks in the hot tub. Downhill skiers have only a short drive to Mount Hood, across the border in Oregon. During the warmer months, rafting on the White Salmon and Klickitat Rivers is a popular pastime, and guided steelhead- and salmon-fishing trips are arranged by the innkeeper.

*Accommodations:* 20 rooms, 19 with private bath. *Driving Instructions:* Take the White Salmon exit off I-84. Cross the toll bridge over theColumbia River and follow the signs to White Salmon. The inn is on the west side of town, on Route 14.

# Index of Inns

## WITH ROOM-RATE AND CREDIT-CARD INFORMATION

Inns are listed in the chart that follows. In general, rates given are for two persons unless otherwise stated. Single travelers should inquire about special rates. The following abbreviations are used throughout the chart:

dbl. = double. These rates are for two persons in a room.

dbl. oc. = double occupancy. These rates depend on two persons being registered for the room. Rentals of the room by a single guest will usually involve a different rate basis.

EP = European Plan: no meals.

MAP = Modified American Plan: rates include dinner and breakfast. Readers should confirm if stated rates are per person or per couple.

AP = American Plan: rates include all meals. Readers should confirm if stated rates are per person or per couple.

BB = Bed and Breakfast: rates include full or Continental breakfast.

### Credit-Card Abbreviations

| | | | |
|---|---|---|---|
| AE = | American Express | MC = | MasterCard |
| CB = | Carte Blanche | V = | Visa |
| DC = | Diners Club | | |

**Important:** All rates are the most recent available but are subject to change. Check with the inn before making reservations.

Camellia Inn, 60; rates: $65 to $115 dbl. BB; MC, V
Captain Whidbey, 243; rates: $55 to $150 dbl. BB; AE, DC, DS, MC, V
Carriage House, 73; rates: $85 to $125 dbl. BB
Carter House Inn, 40; rates: $79 to $199 dbl. BB; AE, MC, V
Casa Laguna Inn, 74; rates: $85 to $205 dbl. BB; AE, DC, DS, MC, V
Casa Madrona Hotel, 161; rates: $90 to $200 dbl. BB; AE, DC, MC, V
Cascade Mountain Inn, 211; rates: $80 dbl. EP; MC, V
Centrella Hotel, 108; rates: $75 to $160 dbl. BB; AE, DC, MC, V
Chambered Nautilus Bed and Breakfast Inn, 235; rates: $59 to $89 dbl. BB; AE,
    MC, V
Channel House, 207; rates: $65 to $80 dbl. BB; MC, V
Chanticleer Bed and Breakfast Inn, 185; rates: $75 to $140 dbl. BB; MC, V
Christmas House Bed and Breakfast Inn, 119; rates: $39 to $115 dbl. BB; DS, MC,
    V
Churchill Manor, 116; rates: $68 to $145 dbl. BB; AE, MC, V
Chichester House Bed and Breakfast, 114; rates: $70 to $75 dbl. BB
City Hotel, 32; rates: $65 to $80 dbl. BB; MC, V
Cliff Crest, 159; rates: $80 to $125 dbl. BB; AE, MC, V
Cobblestone Inn, 25; rates: $95 to $170 dbl. BB; AE, MC, V
College Inn Guest House, 236; rates: $35 to $48 dbl. BB; AE, DC, DS, MC, V
Colonial Inn, 44; rates: $50 to $80 dbl. EP
Columbia Gorge Hotel, 195; rates: $115 to $185 dbl. BB; AE, DC, DS, MC, V
Cooper House Bed and Breakfast Inn, 9; rates: $75 to $80 dbl. BB; MC, V
Country House Inn, 173; rates: $65 to $80 dbl. BB; MC, V
Country Inn, 45; rates: $65 to $105 dbl. BB; AE, MC, V
Court Street Inn, 67; rates: $75 to $150 dbl. BB; AE, MC, V
Culver's, A Country Inn, 20; rates: $95 to $105 dbl. BB
Darling House, 157; rates: $75 to $175 dbl. BB; AE, MC, V
Dehaven Valley Farm Inn, 177; rates: $85 to $125 dbl. BB; AE, MC, V
Doryman's Inn, 105; rates: $135 to $275 dbl. BB; AE, DC, MC, V
Downey House Bed and Breakfast, 219; rates: $65 to $85 dbl. BB; MC, V
Driver Mansion Inn, 123; rates: $75 to $225 dbl. BB; AE, DC, DS, MC, V
Dunbar House, 95; rates: $80 dbl. BB; MC, V
East Brother Light Station, 36; rates: $285 dbl. MAP
Edinburgh Lodge, 187; rates: $75 dbl. BB; MC, V
Edward II Inn, 132; rates: $65 to $85, suites $130 to $200 dbl. BB; AE, MC, V
Elk Cove Inn, 37; rates: $98 to $138 dbl. BB
Fallon Hotel, 33; rates: $50 to $75 dbl. BB; MC, V
Feather Bed Inn, 118; rates: $55 dbl. BB; AE, DC, MC, V
Fensalden, 6; rates: $80 to $125 dbl. BB, lower in off season; MC, V
Fleming Jones Homestead, 115; rates: $80 to $115 dbl. BB
Flying M Ranch, 206; rates: $41 to $145 dbl. EP, AE, DC, DS, MC, V
Foothill House, 21; rates: $85 to $125 dbl. BB; MC, V
Galer Place, 237; rates: $85 dbl. BB; AE, DC, MC, V
Garratt Mansion, 3; rates: $65 to $110 dbl. BB; AE
Gate House Inn, 68; rates: $75 to $105 dbl. BB; MC, V
Gingerbread Mansion, 42; rates: $85 to $165 dbl. BB; MC, V
Glenborough Inn and Cottage, 151; rates: $65 to $155 dbl. BB; AE, MC, V
Glendeven, 76; rates: $70 to $140 dbl., suites higher. BB; MC, V
Gosby House Inn, 109; rates: $85 to $125 dbl. BB; AE, MC, V
Gramma's Bed and Breakfast Inn, 14; rates: $85 to $175 dbl. BB; AE, DC, JCB,
    MC, V
Grandmere's Inn, 102; rates: $95 to $135 dbl. BB; MC, V
Grape Leaf Inn, 61; rates: $70 to $115 dbl. BB; MC, V
Green Gables Inn, 110; rates: $95 to $155 dbl. BB; AE, MC, V
Happy Landing Inn, 27; rates: $90 to $135 dbl. BB; MC, V
Harbor House, 28; rates: $145 to $210 dbl. MAP
Headlands Inn, 82; rates: $89 to $125 dbl. BB
Hearthstone Inn, 192; rates: $55 to $75 dbl. EP; MC, V

### THE COMPLEAT TRAVELER'S READER REPORT

To: *The Compleat Traveler*
c/o Burt Franklin & Co., Inc.
P.O. Box 856
New York, New York 10014, U.S.A.

Dear Compleat Traveler:

I have used your book in _____ (country or region).
I would like to offer the following ☐ new recommendation, ☐ comment,
☐ suggestion, ☐ criticism, ☐ or complaint about:

Name of Country Inn or Hotel:

_____

Address: _____

_____

Comments:

Day of my visit: _____ Length of stay: _____

From (name): _____

Address _____

_____ Telephone: _____